The Cast

The Cast

*Theories and Applications
for More Effective Techniques*

Ed Jaworowski

*With a Foreword
and Photography by
Lefty Kreh*

STACKPOLE
BOOKS

Published by
STACKPOLE BOOKS
Cameron and Kelker Streets
P.O. Box 1831
Harrisburg, PA 17105

Printed in the United States of America

10 9 8 7 6 5 4 3 2 1

First edition

Library of Congress Cataloging-in-Publication Data

Jaworowski, Ed.
   The cast/Ed Jaworowski with a foreword and
photography by Lefty Kreh. — 1st ed.
     p.   cm.
   Includes index.
   ISBN 0-8117-1917-0
   1. Fly casting—Pictorial works. I. Title.
SH454.2.J38   1992   91–27360
                                   CIP

Dedicated to my friend, teacher, and mentor,
Lefty Kreh,
by far the greatest of them all

Contents

Acknowledgments

Many people have contributed to this book. I want to express my sincerest thanks and appreciation particularly to the following:

Lefty Kreh for his direction, coaching, and considerable photographic skills;

Irv Swope for his encouragement as well as his technical and photographic assistance;

Bob Popovics and Bill Dickson for listening, critiquing, and suggesting;

Beth Brodovsky for supplying her artistic talents for illustrations;

Judith Schnell editor, and the staff of Stackpole Books for confidence and patience;

SAGE/Winslow Manufacturing Co. for tackle and other support;

Stan Jurecki for invaluable assistance in so many casting schools;

and to the many students I have been privileged to teach. I hope they have learned as much from me as I have from them.

Foreword

We have been fly casting for several centuries, using techniques developed when anglers used long wooden rods and short, braided horsehair lines to fish small English streams. The system was so inefficient for modern fly fishing situations that the double haul was devised to make up for the shortcomings of this outdated method.

Ed Jaworowski, whom I consider to be the best teacher of fly casting that I have ever known, promotes a modern method of casting, tailored to suit up-to-date tackle and needs.

What is so interesting about Ed's method is that it is so effortless. It allows older people, and those with little strength, to handle heavier tackle and make longer and more difficult casts much more easily than when using the 300-year-old method. A delicate lady angler can easily handle a large tarpon rod and make effective casts with this new method.

Best of all, the method is based on a few simple principles that Ed explains in this book. Using these principles, you can understand what happens during a cast. The principles apply to every cast you'll make. They also help you perceive why you are making good casts and how to correct your casting faults.

Fly fishing calls for more than just the ability to throw a long line—or an accurate one. There are many different kinds of casts to match various fishing situations. With this book Ed helps you master a variety of casts: how to get your fly to the target when there is little room behind you; how to throw a fly around a corner; how to easily toss an extra-high line when there is an obstruction behind you; and how to make an effortless cast when there is a wind to your side. Ed has mastered all of them. If you absorb the contents of this book, you will better understand and enjoy fly casting. It will surely make you a better caster.

Lefty Kreh
Cockeysville, Maryland
December 1990

Introduction

Casting is one of the basic skills required by the sport of fly fishing. Although exact statistics are difficult to establish, there are probably several hundred thousand fly fishers in the United States alone, and their numbers are growing. In terms of fly casting ability, the majority are in the broad, gray area of mediocrity. Most want to cast better, or at least wish they could. The complaints are all too common: "There was too much wind," "I couldn't get a good float with all the currents," or "The bushes limited my casting room." They agonize, "Why does my fly catch the leader when I make my forward cast?" "How come I can't toss a large popping bug even with my heavy line?" "How do I tighten my loop?" "How do I get more distance?" "How can I make my line hook to the right or left?" Such remarks tell me these fishermen aren't casting well under any conditions. When conditions are anything but optimum, they must put up their rods instead of enjoying the variety and fun the sport has to offer.

There are probably as many casts made now for warm- and saltwater species as for trout, and the casting skills that were good enough on a small stream under most conditions just lead to frustration when we broaden our horizons. The fact that so many people have the same complaints indicates that we should look for the solutions in the way fly casting has been taught over the years.

This book was written with these tenets in mind: that the traditional approach to casting instruction has so many built-in shortcomings that it is largely responsible for the many poor and mediocre fly casters, and that there surely is a superior approach to teaching, learning, and understanding fly casting. I am convinced that nearly all casters use too much effort and that fishermen of slight stature, women, even youngsters, possess more than enough strength to cast effectively for long periods of time.

This is not simply another book on casting, using different words to say the same things that have been put forth by a score of other books. It flies in the face of tradition and questions the most basic assertions by which fly casters have lived for generations. At every turn it focuses on the "why" of each technique and deplores any instruction recommended solely on the grounds of tradition. Much of what this book teaches will be judged by my mildest critics as controversial, by my severest as positively heretical. In fact, my explanations will clearly illustrate why so many fishermen have trouble with longer casts, tailing loops, accuracy, casting in the wind, and a dozen other problems. I have written this for all anglers—men, women, and children, novice to advanced—who desire to become better casters.

While it is not necessary to master all the techniques discussed in these pages in order to enjoy fly fishing, every angler will find something that will enhance his or her sport. Nor do I differentiate between fresh and salt water, trout and tarpon. Casting is a mechanical procedure for propelling a fly to a target, regardless of the species waiting at the other end. I have, however, omitted casting with two-handed rods, as such tackle is not yet used extensively in this country.

My technique has been to illustrate four basic principles through high-speed, sequence photography. The text will explain, analyze, or otherwise comment on the casting procedures illustrated in the photos. Along with the recommended strokes, rod positions, and the like, I have included examples of faults and less efficient casting techniques for comparison. I should emphasize that I do not claim my approach is right, as opposed to wrong. Rather, I believe it greatly reduces the caster's effort.

I hope to give the reader a clear, graphic image of what to look for and what to correct in order to make easier, better casts. The basics of this approach to casting are those that Lefty Kreh introduced me to many years ago, and I should like to consider this book a sequel to his 1974 work *Fly Fishing in Salt Water* (Lippincott, Philadelphia). Although the essence of what these pages contain is not original, I have adapted, expanded upon, or otherwise modified his ideas to suit my own approach to teaching. The text also represents a distillation of the information I have gleaned from technical articles on the subject and discussions with professors in the departments of Mechanical Engineering and Physics at Villanova University.

I am quite aware of the liabilities involved in trying to capture action through still photography and of the advances in video formats for such purposes. Nevertheless, still photos and the written text have their place in instruction of this sort. Some may claim, "You can't learn to cast from a book." Without qualifying the sentiment, it probably is true. No one can describe the feel of casting—or the taste of an apple. But then, neither can you learn to tie flies or read a stream or fight big fish from a book. Only in-hand, on-water experience can do any of these things and then only in proportion to the dedication and skill of the student. Still, you can learn about casting, how and why certain principles work, what to look for, and things to ponder and practice. That is the purpose of this book.

Ed Jaworowski
Philadelphia, Pennsylvania
January 1991

1

The Four Principles

The less effort required to make any given cast, the more efficient the cast. Yet "power" has become the accepted approach to casting and "more power" the solution to casting problems. Most people learn to cast by rote, following rigid instructions: "Keep your elbow close to your side; raise the rod to ten o'clock; snap it sharply (the 'power stroke') and stop at one o'clock on the backcast; wait until the line straightens and you feel it tug; strike down hard on the forward cast." Directions like these assure inefficient casting. It's time to rethink clock-face instructions, power strokes, and the like.

I propose to explain casting in terms of four invariable mechanical principles that pertain to every cast, ten feet or one hundred, straight or curved, overhead or roll, backcast or forward cast. I shall discuss them in this chapter, then put them together in subsequent chapters, giving instructions for a wide variety of casts based on the "why" of each technique. The bottom line is always efficiency and ease. Everyone, regardless of how he casts, either uses or abuses these principles. The text will show how to use them and what happens when you abuse them. (For convenience, it also assumes you're a right-handed caster. If you cast with your left hand just reverse the instructions.) You will learn how to make longer casts using less, not more, force, how to make right-angle hook casts easily, how to avoid tailing loops, and much more by continually reapplying the same principles. This is not a series of rigid instructions but a new way to look at casting.

The First Principle

The farther you move the rod, the easier it is to cast.

The fly rod functions as a lever, albeit a complicated one, and, as with any lever, the farther it moves, the more work it does. For a very short cast you may only need to move the rod a very short distance. As the cast length increases or as you need more work from the rod (because of wind or heavy flies, for instance), you must move the rod farther, even to the point of stopping your backcast with the rod nearly parallel to the ground or water behind you. Any time you limit or restrict the length of motion, you must use more force, and mandating that the backcast not go beyond a fixed point, like one o'clock, or that your hand not go beyond your shoulder, is to restrict your motion. Then, as you increase the length of your cast or cast heavier flies or deal with wind, you must apply more and more "power." We now recognize that there is an alternative to using more power: simply move the rod and arm farther. Any time you opt for a shorter motion, you place demands on not only strength but timing and coordination. You also make muscles in the back, shoulder, and arm work harder, which is what makes casting tiring.

When you move your casting hand farther, you distribute the energy you use over a longer distance. If you throw a baseball but never bring your hand back farther than, let's say, your shoulder, you will have to apply a lot of force to throw the ball. It's simply easier if you bring your whole arm back farther and move over an expanded distance. Do the same with a fly rod.

In the photographs showing the arm extended well to the rear when making the longest casts, I am not working harder than I am for the shortest casts. Your basic approach should always be to use as little energy as you can to make any cast. If you can use the same effort for virtually all casts, your muscles will grow accustomed to always expending the same effort. You will almost never get tired and your consistency and accuracy will improve.

Consider this analogy: It requires a very strong man to lift five hundred pounds, but a small boy can do it (although he will take longer) if he moves it ten pounds at a time. The same amount of total energy is expended for the job, but the boy is never required to apply the force the man is. So it is with the fly rod. If you make a long stroke, you are using up the same amount of energy over a longer time and distance; it's easier in the sense that you never apply a lot of force at any point.

That is precisely why you probably have little difficulty in casting twenty to thirty feet but can't make long casts or do a lot of other things with a fly rod. "I can cast well at close range, but I can't make long casts or use heavy tackle" is a common remark. You cast well at short range because the short distance you move the casting hand is sufficient. Yet to maintain a stroke of the same length and try to cast farther, you must use more force, your timing must be flawless, and, if there is any slack in the line, you have little opportunity to remove it before making the cast. Not only will you require more effort if you use a shorter backcast, you will have allowed less forward travel for your forward cast, meaning more force must also be applied in that direction. This is the reason we hear so much about "power" and "power strokes." I decry the use of "power" at any phase of the cast.

On a very short cast you might not have to stop farther back than this, but only the length of the cast determines the stopping point. There is no specific point at which to stop the backcast.

A slightly longer cast may call for a stop at this point.

To make a longer cast, stop here.

Still longer, stop here.

Longer yet, about here.

For maximum distance with the same amount of effort, put your arm well back. An added advantage is that such movement extends the leverage of the cast to your hips.

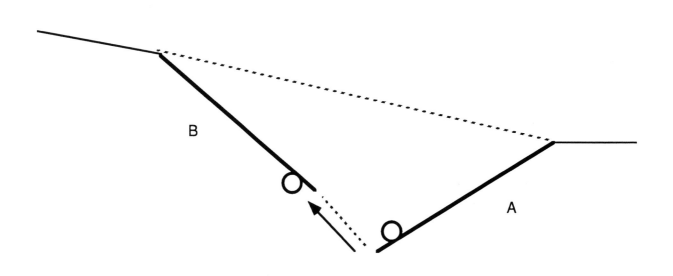

If on the backcast the rod is well back and low (A), the arm and rod can rise when making a longer cast (B), which is a natural motion.

When you want to cast farther, just as in shooting or throwing a ball, you must aim higher. When you make a longer cast, you will actually use a shorter forward stroke because you stop sooner or higher. So add motion to the rear that you removed from the front.

If you cast with a short, hammerlike stroke, you have limited distance potential, unless you use a lot of power. Let me emphasize that I am not just discussing distance. I'm concerned about being able to make the same casts you now make but making them more easily, that is, with a more efficient use of the energy in the cast. Thinking in terms of these principles will enable you to make casts you never imagined and to meet many fishing challenges that used to frustrate you.

Don't be concerned about your elbow; deliberately keeping it close to your side, when a longer stroke requires it to move, obviously only inhibits your motion. Insisting that you keep your elbow close to your side, like insisting your backcast never go beyond some predetermined point, will only compel you to use more force in your limited range of motion. On a shorter cast your elbow will perhaps be close to your side, but as the cast lengthens it will move away. The point is that the elbow should not be rigid. Let it move, bend, and flex if it has to, responding to where you move the rod and your hand. In fishing situations you will have to deal with wind conditions, trees, and other obstacles, and you will note throughout this book that many of the casts designed to meet these challenges compel you to move your elbow from your side.

What about drifting after you stop the rod on the backcast? Some insist upon it but I see no need for this extra motion. Why stop the rod at point A and then move it farther to point B? Simply stop at point B in the first place, which incidentally means a longer, and hence easier, backcast. In addition to being unnecessary, drifting the rod, unless perfectly timed and coordinated, can actually cause the backcast loop to open, making the cast deteriorate. Rod drift is not like the follow-through of golf or tennis. Imagine what would happen if a taut string were attached to the golf ball when you followed through.

The Second Principle
You can't make the cast until you make the end of the line move.
Consider this: If you tied a lure to the end of a spinning line and left ten feet of slack between the tip of the rod and the lure, you obviously couldn't cast. There would be no resistance to cause the rod tip to bend and load—not until all the slack were removed and the lure started to move. Similarly, until you make the end of your fly line move, the rod can never have the full weight of the line against which to load. Therefore, instructions like raising the rod to ten o'clock and snapping it to one o'clock will not give you a good cast unless you first get the end of the line moving. Any time you move the rod tip and the end of the line doesn't move, you have wasted energy, so you must supply more if you are to make the same cast.

My first recommendation is to start with the rod tip low, to minimize the slack. The line needn't be perfectly straight on the water before you cast although it is desirable to have it so if possible. If there is only a small amount of slack on the water, the longer stroke already recommended will remove it in short order and still leave you with plenty of distance to load the rod and make the cast. If you have a lot of slack on the water, you may opt to strip in most of it before beginning the backcast so that the end of the line will move as soon as the rod tip starts to move. If the slack is piled close to you and you find that stripping it all in will not leave you with enough to make a good backcast, roll-cast the line straight, then make a normal backcast. Or you can switch the tip back and forth, setting the line moving until the end of the line starts to move, then make a backcast, or just let the current straighten it out if facing downstream. In short, do whatever it takes to get that whole line moving. You can't load the rod until you do, and it is inefficient to waste part of the casting stroke just pulling out slack.

A backcast is simply a forward cast going in the opposite direction, so the principle works exactly the same when you make your forward cast. If you have a big looping backcast, for example, as you come forward the rod tip may move four feet while the end of the line may move only four inches. Highly inefficient. The last chapter will expand on this and similar problems.

I should add here that the backcast does not load the rod for the forward cast. Many casters believe that if they cast harder on the backcast, they will somehow store energy for the forward cast. In fact, the rod loads when it moves to the rear and unloads when it stops. It then loads and unloads again on the forward cast. They are two separate and distinct casts. A loaded rod will cast line simply by recoiling and straightening. If the backcast could load the rod, it should therefore be possible to make a backcast, stop the rod, and have the recoil cast the line forward. This will not happen.

The point to remember is that when the end of the line starts moving, the entire weight of the fly line outside the rod tip offers resistance to the moving rod and can load

One of the most common casting problems is starting the pickup with the rod aimed high so that the tip is at eye level or above.

When you begin the pickup keep the rod tip low—below your belt line—with the rod and line in as straight a line as possible. Make this a habit.

it. As long as some slack exists, some of the rod's motion will be wasted just taking up the slack, and the rod can't load until all of it is gone.

In a typical cast when you start with the rod low to the water and the line and rod in a virtual straight line, you ensure two things: you allow yourself a longer stroke; and as soon as you begin to raise the rod, the end of the line starts to move so no motion is wasted and you get an efficient, effortless backcast. It is then difficult to understand why you should do something different when making the forward cast. Specifically the rod and line position to the rear, as you start your forward cast, should mimic the position they were in when you started your backcast and for precisely the same reasons—you are allowing yourself to make a longer stroke, and every inch the tip moves forward it will be moving the end of the fly line.

The longer the cast, the more important it is to start with the rod tip low. Here the tip is lowered to the water for a rather long pickup and cast.

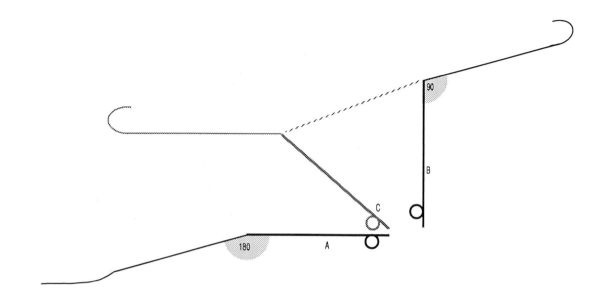

With the rod low (A) you begin your backcast nearly in a 180-degree alignment. But if you stop your backcast just beyond vertical (B), you will start your forward cast with the rod and line at around 90 degrees, meaning you must use more effort because the length of the forward cast (to C) is quite short.

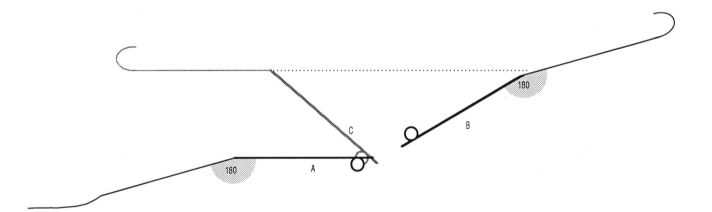

Here the starting points of the backcast (A) and the forward cast (B) are the same. A longer stroke (to C) is also allowed. The same Principle holds true in both directions.

The Third Principle
Continuously accelerate, then stop the rod.
Let's start with a few more comments about loading the rod. On the forward cast the rod loads when you move the butt end forward and the weight of the line or lure holds the tip back. When the hand stops the butt end of the rod, the bent rod rapidly straightens and projects the line or lure. Clearly, if there is excess slack between the rod tip and the lure (in the case of spinning) or the end of the line (in the case of fly casting), the rod can't get properly loaded and you waste much of your motion. Likewise, if the tip moves forward at the same rate as the hand, the rod can't load. Therefore once you make the end of the line move, you must continually accelerate your hand until you stop the rod.

The actual casting motion is one smooth, progressive acceleration followed by an abrupt stop. If you think in terms of snapping, punching, or suddenly applying power, you will work harder and often get slack or shock waves in your line. Those waves represent wasted energy. No part of the casting stroke should be at a constant speed. Even though you may be moving the rod fast, unless it is getting faster all the time, the rod will not load deeply and little energy will reach the end of the line. If you start moving your hand slowly and continually get faster with a very short, rapid acceleration at the end and then stop the rod, you will make an efficient stroke, even though you are aware of little effort. The diagram on the next page should give you some idea of what I mean by the final acceleration, or "speed-up and stop."

Try this: Lay the fly line on the grass, straight out to the rear with the rod tip straight back so that it aims directly down the fly line. This ensures that you are complying with the first two principles when you come forward, namely, that you will move the rod tip a long distance (fifteen to twenty feet), and you will be moving the end of the line right from the start—no motion is wasted just removing slack.

This position should guarantee a good, effortless forward cast. However, if you make a sudden, fast, powerful forward cast with all your strength, the line will go forward weakly, fail to straighten, stop, and pile up. What happened to all the energy you put into the cast? Why didn't it end up at the end of the fly line, giving a long cast? You violated the Third Principle. When you came forward, you were moving your hand at maximum speed virtually from the first instant. From that point until the time you stopped the forward motion, the rod was going fast, but it wasn't accelerating. The rod did not get deeply loaded, so when it straightened it never developed maximum tip speed to throw the line the whole distance.

Now repeat the cast. This time, however, begin very slowly, constantly increase the speed (so that the motion of your hand is very rapid only in the last few inches), and abruptly stop the rod. The line will shoot forward and straighten out. Using only a fraction of the effort used on the first attempt, you got much better results.

The Fourth Principle
The line will go in the direction the tip was moving when it stopped.
What does this mean in terms of your fishing? If you want to cast higher (for distance), lower (under brush), or around an obstacle, make certain the tip stops while it is moving

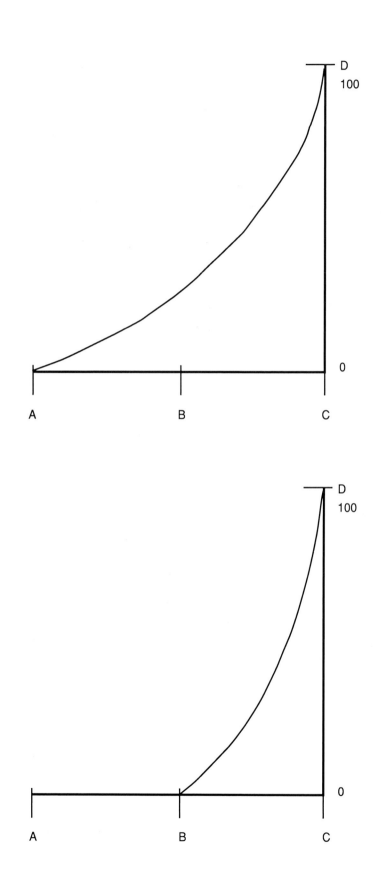

This diagram suggests the longer stroke and more gradual acceleration I recommend. While moving from A to B, your hand continues to get faster throughout the stroke. You distribute the energy over a longer time.

If you use a short stroke you must accelerate over a shorter distance, which means more force. Timing is also more critical. This represents the kind of effort you must use with a shorter stroke.

A constant, smooth acceleration will result in a deeply loaded rod. Here the final part of the acceleration is reached and I am about to stop the rod.

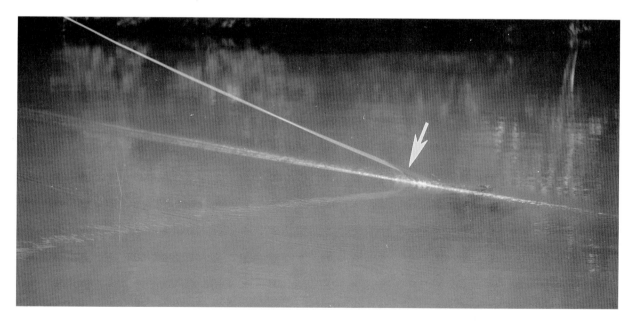

Regardless of how much line you pick up off the water, you should always reach your quick, final acceleration (what some call the "power stroke") just as the end of the line starts to leave the surface, regardless of the position of the rod.

Contrary to some claims, the line will not go down if the rod stopped well back on the backcast, as long as the rod tip was moving in an upward direction when it stopped.

Notice that the line continues to move in the direction the tip was moving when it stopped.

upward, downward, or in a curve. It is that simple. Conversely, it is obvious that if your line came down in a curve when you wanted it to go straight, you must have pushed slightly to the side when you accelerated and stopped, causing the tip to stop in that direction.

How often have you been told that "You brought your rod back too far" when you made a backcast? When most people see the rod stopped well back and the line hitting the water, they assume that the former caused the latter. Yet, getting the rod well back is often desirable. I have already pointed out that the farther back the rod stops, the easier both the backcast and the forward cast will be; you really can't bring the rod back too far. What matters is not how far back the rod is but rather how it got there—whether the tip was moving downward or upward when it stopped. That's all. Learn to study the line. It tells everything you need to know to improve your casting. When the rod stops, note the direction of the first few feet of line coming out from the tip-top. They indicate the direction from which the tip was coming.

The ramifications of this principle are marvelous for the angler. The instant you appreciate its full import, you will understand how to cast hooks to the right or left, avoid tailing loops, make casts straight ahead with no backcast room, and solve dozens of problems that now affect your fishing.

The only two reasons I have heard advanced for stopping the rod abruptly at a point no farther back than one o'clock are that it will load the rod (a ridiculous claim we have already dispelled), and that putting the rod back will make the line go down to the water or ground behind you, which is equally absurd, for this will only happen if the rod tip is moving downward when it stops.

To demonstrate that it is the casting technique, not the length of the rod, that makes the backcast hit the water behind you, a cast is made here with only the tip section of a fly rod. Note that the rod has stopped pointed well back, yet the line is not going downward.

Most fishermen assume that if they are wading deep, fishing from a bellyboat, or have bushes or a sand dune behind them, they must use a longer rod to prevent the line from slapping the water on the backcast or catching on an obstacle. Resorting to the purchase of another, longer rod is skirting the problem, not correcting it. Although longer rods do have advantages in many situations, you should solve your casting problem first. In fact, to emphasize the point that it is the poor cast, not the length of the rod, that makes the line hit the water, here is a cast made with only the tip section of the rod. Note that the rod is stopped well back but the line still doesn't hit the water.

Always think in terms of this principle when you select the direction you want the line to go. It is invariable. Conversely, if the line goes where you least wanted it to, you know where to look for the cause. When fishing you face endless variables. If a tree stands twenty feet to your rear, stopping the rod at one o'clock will assure disaster, so you may decide to stop (by "stabbing" the rod) at three o'clock in order to make the line go under the lowest branches. When someone asks me, "Where do you stop your backcast?" my standard reply is to ask for more information. I ask, "Where do I want the line to go?" or "Where are the trees?"

Keep in mind that all casts are made essentially the same way: *Make the end of the line move, continually accelerate, then stop the rod so that the tip stops while it is moving in the direction you want the line to go, moving the rod and arm farther whenever you need help, either for distance, wind, or heavier flies.* Always strive to employ as little effort as possible. Practice casting according to these principles, and as you gradually master each one, you will be amazed at how effortless fly casting can be.

2

The Basic Cast

It will be helpful to most people to understand that the mechanics of fly casting are the same as those of spin or bait casting, even surf casting. Some anglers claim otherwise, but anyone thoroughly versed in all these methods realizes that the same actions, though modified, take place. Certainly the Four Principles apply. Without getting into a discussion of rod actions and types, I shall only say that modern graphite rods, even many inexpensive models, will perform more satisfactorily than rods of other materials—even early graphites. No casting instruction can make a poor rod better, so I advise you to use a graphite rod from a reputable maker. You will more quickly master casting if you are not hampered by poor equipment.

Getting Started
Some Preliminary Notes
One of the true ironies of fly casting is that you must already have some line out in front of you before you can make a cast. One of the biggest problems for the absolute beginner is just how to get the thirty feet or so of line out in the first place so that he can start casting. If working on the grass, you can simply lay the rod down and pull off line, laying it out straight, or have someone else walk it off. You can try gently wiggling the rod back and forth while gradually letting extra line slip out from the left hand and then backing off until it is straight. On water with a slow current, simply let the current pull the line out below you. The roll cast described in the next chapter is best of all.

Always make certain that you have a leader attached to the fly line when you practice casting. A tiny piece of brightly colored yarn tied to the end helps you keep track of the cast but is not necessary. Finally, I strongly advise that you watch your backcast when you are learning to cast. Many instructors preach against this habit, but I have found that most fly casters respond faster and make better progress if they can see exactly what happens back there. You can't change things until you can see what is wrong.

Grip, Hands, Stance

Before you begin the cast, place your thumb on top of the rod grip with the guides hanging straight down. The thumb acts as a rudder for directional control in addition to providing a secure, solid grip. When you grasp the handle of the rod, the thumb and index finger of the casting hand support the rod. The other fingers simply caress the rod gently and help balance it. Don't squeeze hard.

I strongly advise against casting with the index finger extended along the grip. This is a weaker grip, and you tend to hold the rod between the middle, ring, and little fingers and the heel of the hand. This requires a tighter squeeze, gives control that is less sure, places the fulcrum for the leverage a few inches lower (contrary to assumptions, the tip of the little finger, not the index finger, usually becomes the fulcrum), and calls for the use of more strength. Additionally, as you will see later, more control for a variety of casts can be achieved with the thumb on top.

Similarly, some people cast with the thumb off to the side in a V grip. This is better than the extended index finger grip but makes it difficult to control loops and execute some of the practical fishing casts to be discussed.

When making longer casts, you must turn the hand as you reach back, and it may be more comfortable to turn the back of the hand slightly outward to the right (for a right-handed caster) before starting the pickup. This places the guides slightly to the left but has no adverse affect upon the cast. This makes it easier to keep the wrist straight during the pickup and easier to point the tip in the direction you want the line to go.

The left hand is as important as the right in many respects. The main function of the left hand is to keep the line tight between itself and the butt, or stripping, guide. Don't allow the hands to get widely separated during the cast. In normal casting, the distance between the hands should remain constant or you will create slack, greatly reducing efficiency. Move the left hand slightly, following the right hand on the backcast and leading on the forward cast.

Stance is important for comfort and efficiency in casting. If casting with the right hand, stand with the right foot slightly back so that the arm can reach back naturally and not feel awkward and restricted. As when throwing a ball, shooting an arrow, or performing many other athletic motions, the body will not perform naturally and comfortably facing straight ahead, feet square to the target—although for very short, close-in casts, such a position may be acceptable. With a stance that is slightly more closed, as golfers call it (that is, with the body slightly turned and the right foot pulled back), the body can flow and move with the motion of the cast, balance is better, and the caster is more comfortable. On longer casts this position also allows the hips to become the fulcrum of your motion; this gives tremendous mechanical advantage.

This grip gives maximum control. Place the thumb on top of the grip. The thumb and the index finger actually hold the rod. The other three fingers gently wrap around the grip and control the rod. Don't squeeze with these fingers.

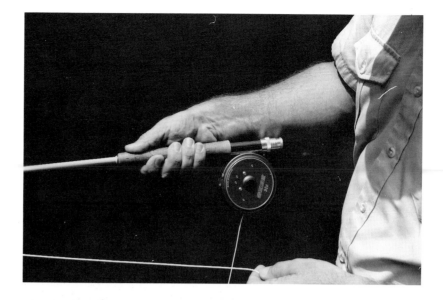

The V-grip (with the thumb to the side) gives less strength and control. It also tends to make most casters squeeze the grip with the three back fingers.

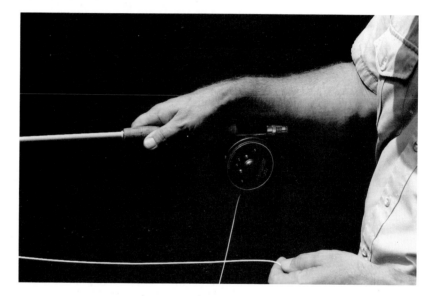

Laying the index finger along the top of the grip is the poorest grip of all. Leverage, strength, accuracy, and control all suffer.

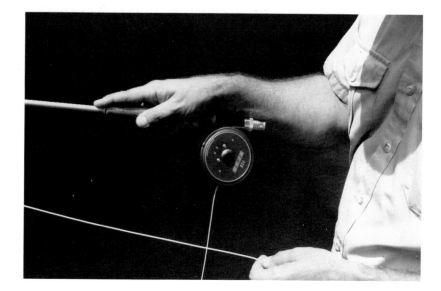

For moderate to long casts, with the thumb on top and the rod tip low, before you start your back cast . . .

. . . turn the hand to the side so that the guides face to the side as shown.

This position makes it feel natural and comfortable to reach the arm back for longer casts.

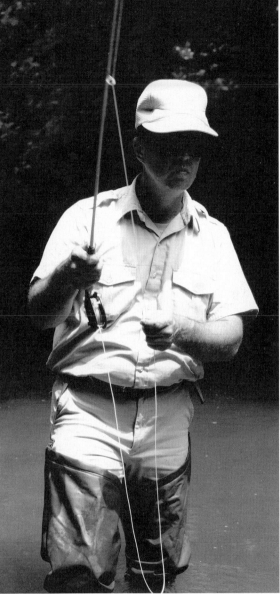

During the pickup, maintain a constant distance between the hands.

On the forward cast they should remain in approximately the same positions in relation to each other, unless hauling, as explained later.

For all but very short casts, turning slightly to the side so that the left foot is forward makes it easier to reach your arm back.

Making a Cast Applying the Four Principles

This sequence shows one complete cast, pickup, backcast, and forward cast with photographs taken at high speed. Move your eyes quickly from one photo to the next, noting the time lapse for each phase of the cast.

This sequence shows one complete cast, pickup, backcast, and forward cast taken at six frames per second. Let your eyes follow the rod and arm through the sequence, sensing the slow start and quick final acceleration on the backcast, then do the same for the forward cast.

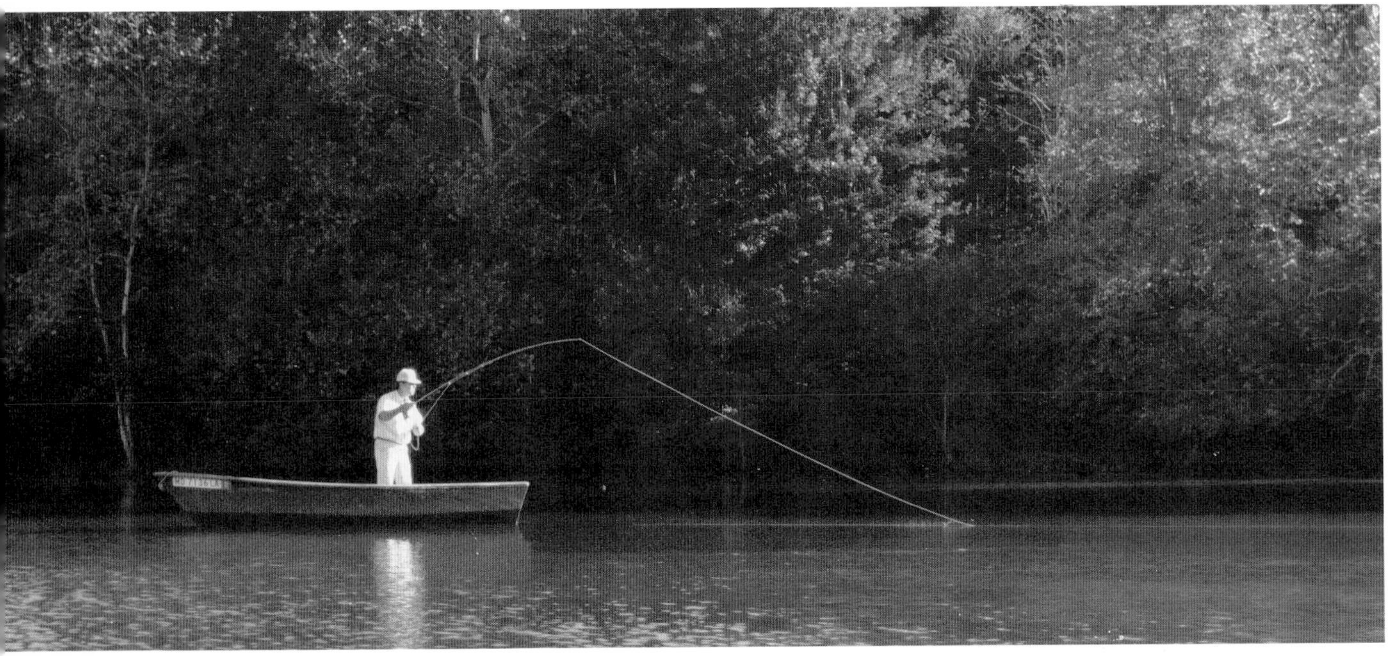

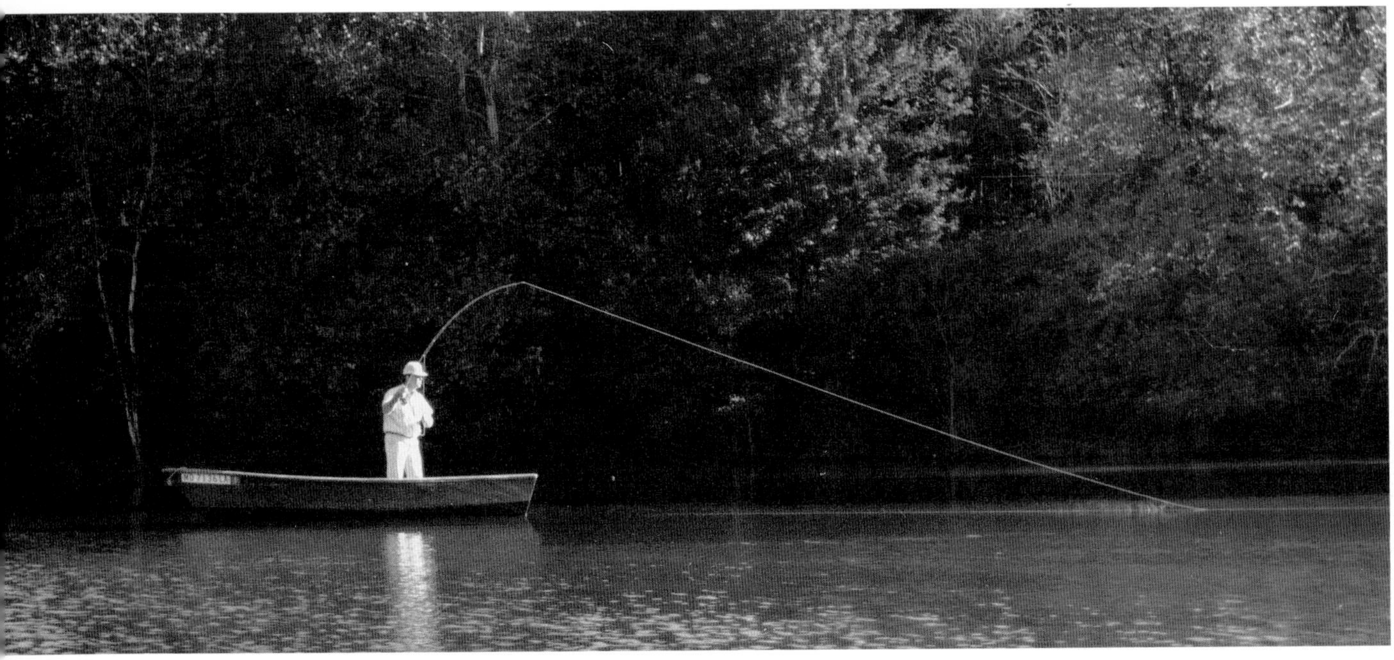

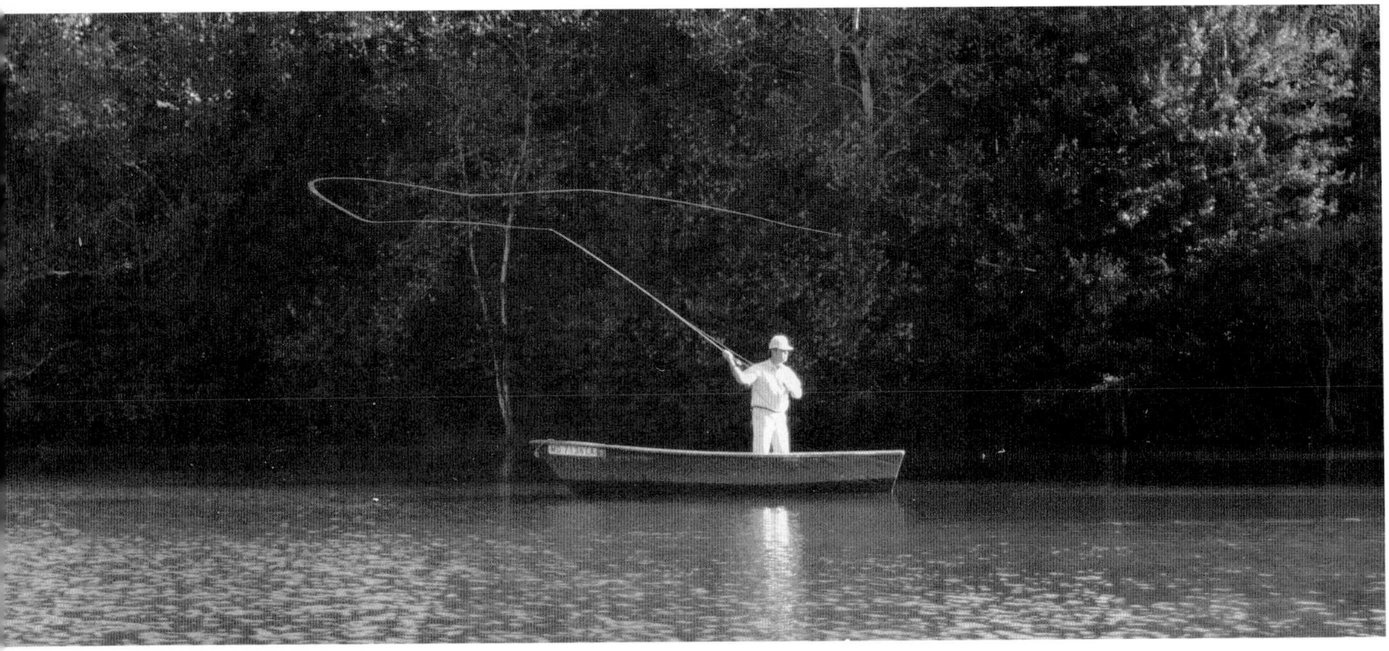

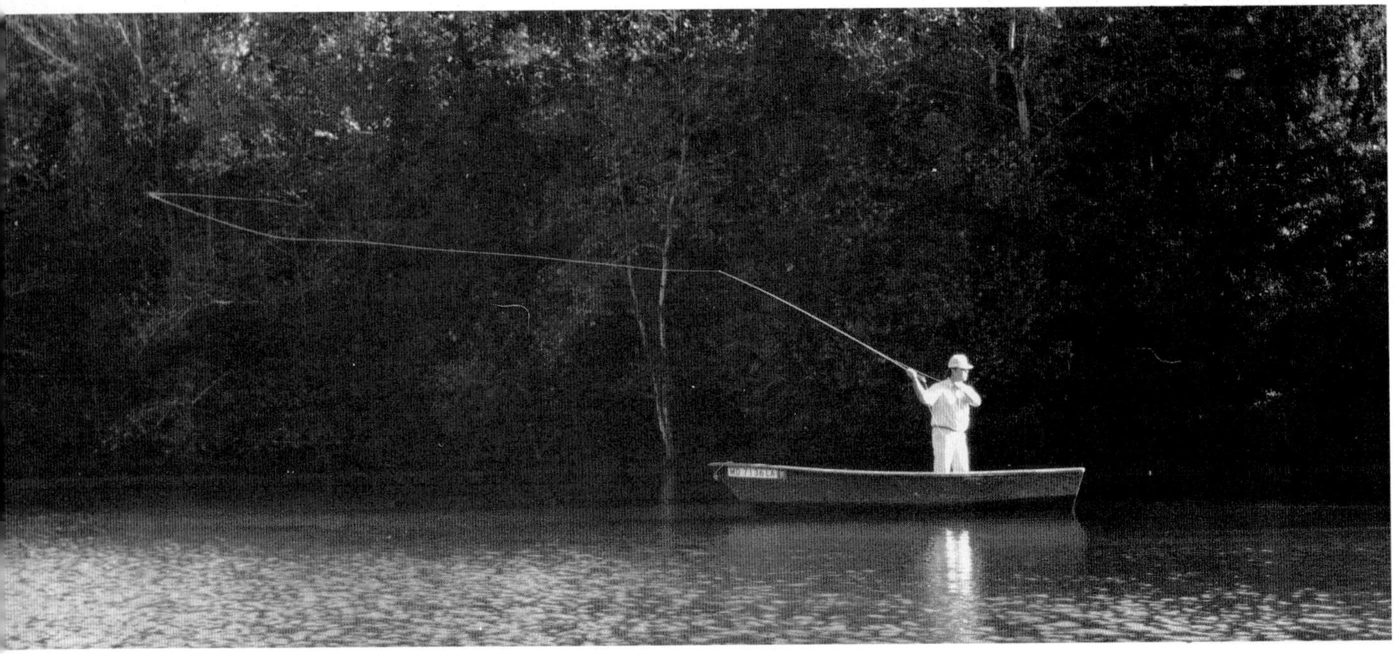

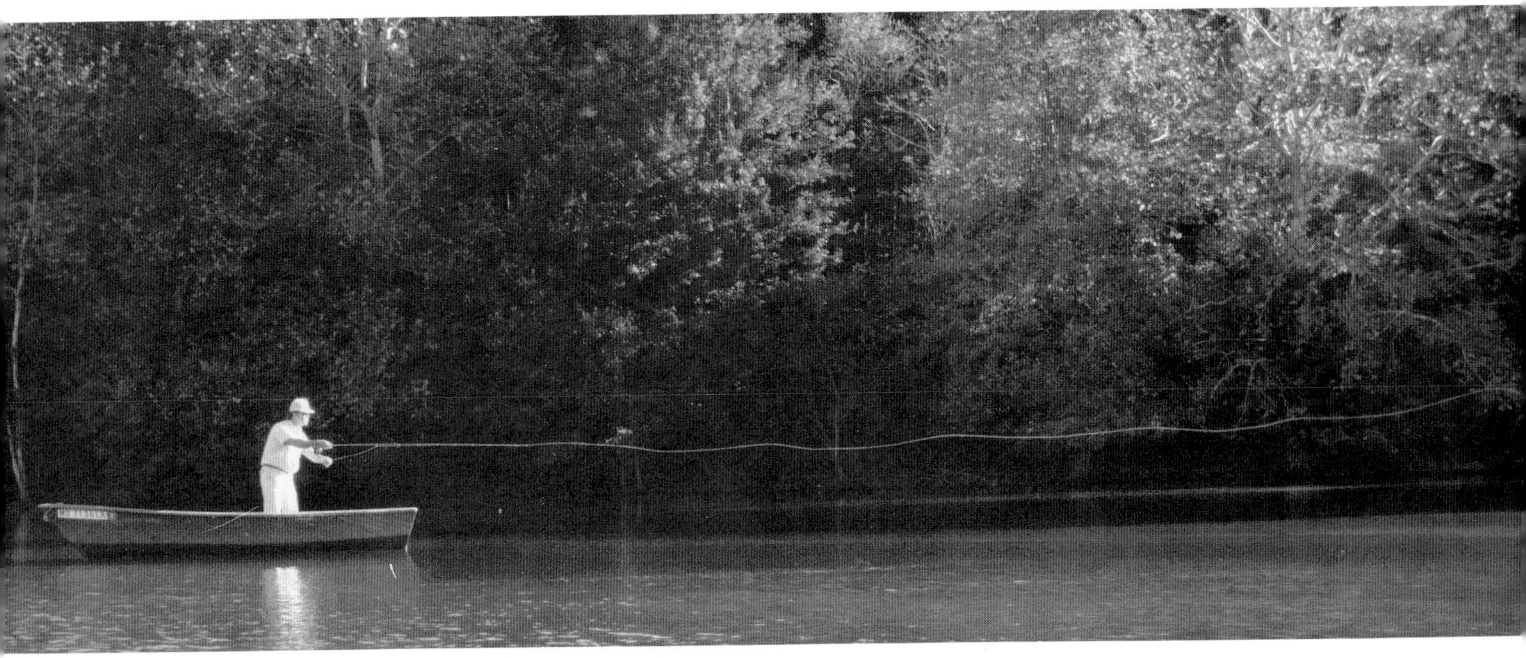

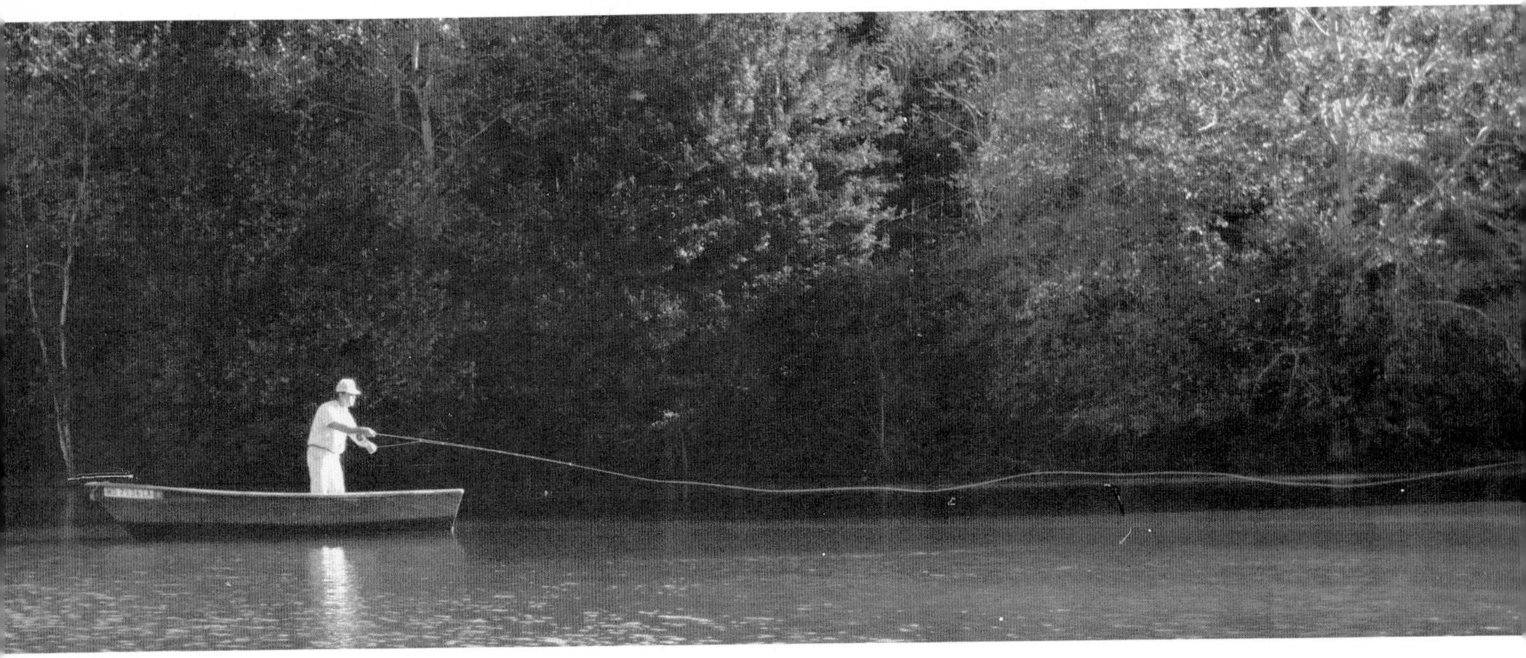

Here is a close-up, step-by-step analysis of a similar cast, shot at the same speed. Key items to note: low starting position; slow start increasing to a very quick and short final acceleration; rod and hand stopping well back and no drifting after the stop; and forward cast starting slowly and finishing with a similar final acceleration and stop.

The rod tip is low, the rod and fly line in a straight line.

Start raising the rod slowly.

Continue moving the rod without bending the wrist.

Continue,
getting a little
faster.

The whole
line is now off
the water
and its weight
has the rod
loaded.

The final
acceleration,
just a few
inches, comes
into play.
Notice the
hand speed at
this point.

The rod is stabbed backward and slightly upward. No energy is applied to the backcast after this point. (The arm and rod would not be so far back for a shorter cast.)

The loop is unrolling to the rear. No drift or additional motion is necessary.

The line continues to straighten. Note there is no change in the caster's position . . .

. . . as the line continues to straighten.

Just before the line straightens completely (it resembles a J or a candy cane), the rod hand starts to move forward slowly, then continues to move faster, just as in the backcast.

The brief, quickest part of the acceleration occurs as the hand comes into the caster's peripheral vision.

The rod is stopped with the tip moving slightly upward. No energy is applied after this point. Note that a shorter cast would be aimed a little lower.

The rod is aimed in the direction the line is traveling.

When the line straightens and begins to fall, the rod is lowered slowly to the fishing position.

Here is a look at the entire cast from the front. Note that the planes of the back and forward casts needn't be, in fact shouldn't be, the same. They are actually two separate and distinct casts, and I have intentionally emphasized the separation here. The backcast is made more to the side than is the forward cast, where the rod is more vertical.

The rod is being raised slowly, lifting the line from the water.

The rod continues to move a bit faster all the time.

When the last inch of fly line starts to leave the water, the very short, quick acceleration comes in and . . .

. . . the stop propels the line rearward.

As the line forms a loop and unrolls . .

. . . the caster waits. Notice there is no drift or other motion necessary.

Just before the loop completely straightens, slowly start the forward motion.

The quick speed-up and stop forms the loop and sends the line on its way. The back and forward casts do not have to travel in the same planes. No energy is applied after this point.

The rod tip is pointed in the direction the line is traveling to minimize drag through the guides.

As the line
straightens
out a few feet
above the
water . . .

. . . and starts
to fall, the
rod follows it
down . . .

. . . to the
fishing
position.

Loop Control

A tight loop is formed by stopping the rod high. The final acceleration was very brief and the tip finished in a straight line.

Varying the size of the casting loop involves, above all else, controlling the direction of the final tip movement. You should practice stopping the rod at various points so that you can vary the loop size at will to meet different tackle and fishing requirements.

Compare the wide loop to the rotation of a bicycle tire, throwing off some of its energy in tangents to the general direction of travel. You can then liken the narrow loop to the flight of an arrow, in which virtually all the energy is expended straight ahead.

Close-up of the same stopping position.

A wider loop is caused by stopping the rod lower. The final acceleration was longer and the rod tip finished while traveling in a more curved path.

A closer look at the stop position.

Stopping the rod much lower—a longer final acceleration with the tip finishing while going downward—will produce a very wide loop.

Close-up of the stopping position for a very wide loop.

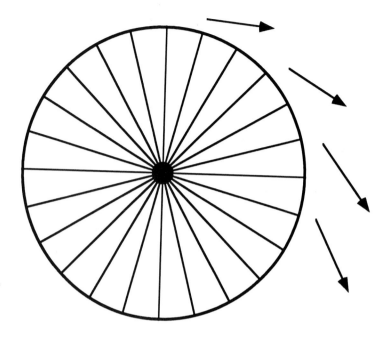

A wide casting loop throws off energy in different directions.

A narrow casting loop focuses energy in one direction.

Horizontal Cast

Often trees or other obstructions will prevent you from making your back and forward casts overhead. There is no essential difference between an overhead and a horizontal cast. Simply make all the same motions described above but move the rod backward and forward parallel to the water. Few anglers have any difficulty making this minor adjustment.

Over the Opposite Shoulder (Backhand Cast)

You should be able to cast at any angle, horizontal to vertical on the right or the left. Here I show a cast made over the left shoulder with the right hand. Cast as for the conventional cast illustrated earlier, except that the casting hand has some limit to its motion and the rod comes back over the opposite shoulder. You will generally find it more comfortable to adjust your stance so that your right foot is somewhat forward, rather than your left.

You can make a similar cast by keeping your hand on the right, as for the normal cast, but tipping the rod tip well over to the left. You will have to bend your body and head to the left, however, to get out of the way of the rod, which I find more awkward. Whichever technique you use, make certain that the knuckles of the casting hand are facing toward the target at all times. Although this cast is sometimes referred to as a "backhand cast," avoid casting with the back of the hand facing away from you, and thus sacrificing some control and accuracy.

The cast is performed the same as the normal cast illustrated earlier, except with the palm of the rod hand always facing forward as shown in close-up photos on the following pages.

If you make a backcast over the opposite shoulder, maintain this position—with the knuckles facing the target when you come forward.

When you make the
forward cast with the back
of the hand facing the
target, control and accuracy
usually suffer.

False Casting

You can make a series of back and forward casts without letting the line fall to the water. This is usually done to extend the line, by letting a little line slip through your left hand on the forward and backcasts, or to dry a floating fly that has absorbed some water. Aside from these, discipline yourself to use as few false casts as possible. One backcast followed by one forward cast is the ideal toward which you should strive. Excessive false casting is a detriment to good fishing technique.

Make a normal pickup, acceleration, stop, and . . .

. . . backcast.

Make your forward cast, but before the line straightens completely . . .

. . . make another backcast.

Now make your final forward cast and let the line fall to the water.

3

Roll Casts

For years we have been instructed to make a roll cast by first raising the rod about straight up, then striking down hard at the water while the line is still moving toward us. This is an inefficient technique; it requires power and line tends to pile up at the end if you do try to cast more easily. It makes little sense to throw the line downward when you want it to go forward.

There is certainly a better way. The Four Principles discussed earlier hold true for the roll cast with one variation. To reiterate: The farther the rod and arm move, the easier the cast; the actual cast is a constant acceleration from a very slow start, dramatically increasing for a few inches prior to the stop; and the direction the tip is moving when it stops determines the direction the line will go.

The variation? If you are casting a floating line, when you raise the rod and point it back preparatory to making the roll, the cast should *not* be made until the line on the water stops moving toward you. There is logic behind this apparent contradiction. Normally we make the end of the line move prior to making a backcast in order to be sure we are not trying to cast slack line, so when the end of the line starts to move, we know the rod is pulling against the whole weight of the line. Again, the line provides the resistance, or load, to the rod that is necessary to make the cast. Similarly, we try to eliminate any slack before making the forward cast so that as the rod moves forward, the weight of the line behind us puts a load on the rod tip. In roll casting, however, it is surface tension created by the line on the water that provides most of the resistance. When the rod is raised and the line slides across the water toward the caster surface, tension is minimal, and if the caster comes forward before the line stops moving, he is trying to cast the slack that is being fed toward the rod tip. You can make the cast but you must use extra force.

Note too, that whereas there are may only be six feet of line in contact with the surface in a given cast when you make the forward stroke, if you do nothing but wait a second or two for the line to stop, when you come forward there will be about fifteen feet of line in contact with the surface. This is far more efficient because the rod loads more readily with the increased resistance. In the case of a sinking line, you must start your roll cast while it is still moving slightly. The water will supply plenty of resistance to load the rod, and if you wait, the line will sink and actually provide too much resistance for an easy roll cast.

It is the amount of line on the water close to the caster that provides most of the resistance to the rod tip when making the roll cast. Therefore, the line should hang down from the tip right to the water at the caster's feet or slightly behind him. When making the actual casting stroke, the rod should (just as in the normal forward cast) be coming from a position pointing to the rear, not straight up, and the forward stroke goes not down toward the water but out and away from the caster. In fact the roll-cast stroke, to be efficient and easy, should be exactly the same as the regular forward stroke, for that is what it is.

By starting with the hand back farther and the rod pointed much farther back, you can allow for a much longer stroke; hence less effort is used for the same cast.

The hand moves forward, just as in a normal forward cast. The line is directed the way you want the cast to go, not down at the water immediately in front of you.

The cast finished with the rod tip going out and away from the caster. Nearly all the energy is put into the forward direction of the cast.

The loop continues to unroll above the water.

Once the end of the line, the leader, and fly turn over . . .

. . . the line straightens and falls to the water in a delicate presentation.

Advocating a high starting position (e.g., the rod at twelve o'clock), and/or a hard downward stroke toward the water, and/or starting the cast before the line stops all require more force. Most of the energy is driven down into the water. If you cast as I recommend, most of the energy is directed forward—the direction you want to cast.

With few exceptions, the roll cast should be made in the air, not on the water. It makes for a more delicate presentation and you can shoot line. Tighten the loop on your roll cast precisely as in the normal forward cast, as discussed in the preceding chapter. There will be times when you need a tight roll—wind, overhang, etc. Finally, don't assume roll casts should be nearly vertical. Practice casting with the rod in the horizontal position, too, and all angles in between.

Using Roll Casts

The first, and often the only, claim made for the roll cast is that you can use it when backcast room is limited. True, but this is only the beginning. In fact, in some tight situations there are better moves to employ than the roll cast. So what else can you do with a roll cast? You can use it to get line out before you actually start fishing. Simply strip a little line off the reel and shake the rod tip back and forth so that it falls outside the tip-top. Then make a short roll to straighten it. Strip a little more line, shake it out, and roll again. Once you have fifteen or twenty feet of line on the water in front of you, you can make your normal backcast and forward cast.

If a very strong wind from the rear makes it difficult to make a good backcast, don't fight it by resorting to whipping or snapping the cast forward. Eliminate the backcast entirely. After all, the only purpose for the backcast is to get the line in some position so that the rod tip can load against it as you make the forward cast. In such conditions, you may be able to simply use the roll cast, letting the wind help push it forward. As stated above, the roll cast is simply the forward cast. Here are other applications.

Horizontal Roll Cast

When overhead branches restrict your normal roll cast, or when casting to a target far back under an overhang, make the loop travel horizontally. The rod tip should finish at the same height above the water at which it started.

Roll Cast in a Crosswind

If a strong wind is pushing from your rod-hand side, as you raise the rod the wind will push a belly into your line in front of you. Casting without tangling may be difficult.

The solution to this problem rests in keeping the wind from blowing the line around. Don't expose the line to the wind until just before you make the forward stroke.

To emphasize the three most important points for an easier roll cast: The cast starts well to the rear . . .

. . . the cast is made straight ahead . . .

. . . and the line rolls out in the air.

Keep the rod tip low as you bring the rod back to the rear. When the rod is well to the rear, stop for an instant until the line stops moving toward you.

Simply make a horizontal forward cast. Without bending the wrist, start coming forward, slowly then more markedly accelerating.

As with a normal overhead cast, when your casting hand comes just into your peripheral vision, you should be at the final acceleration.

Speed up and stop
the tip parallel to the
water, not pointing
downward.

The water tension
will form the line
into a tight low loop.

The line will
lay out under any
overhanging
obstacles.

A common problem. When the caster raises the rod to make a roll cast, a strong wind from his right may billow the line across his body so that a normal roll cast will tangle.

Here's how to defeat the wind. Keep the rod tip very low—nearly touching the water—so that the wind cannot blow it to your left.

Keep the rod tip in that position as you draw it back.

When the rod is pointed well to the rear . . .

. . . start to raise the rod tip. Don't apply any energy yet.

Note that no speed-up has occurred and the wrist is not bent; you are simply lining up to make a regular roll cast.

Continue to raise the rod to the same position as you would normally and pause a second for the line to stop moving toward you.

Make a normal roll cast by starting slowly and continuing to accelerate.

As the rod approaches the vertical position you should be approaching the final acceleration.

Stop the rod so the tip stops while going straight ahead (not downward).

The rod is stabilized while the line continues to unroll.

Here the last part of the loop is straightening out.

Roll Cast Over the Opposite Shoulder (Backhand Roll)

Often you'll need to make the cast from the opposite side of your body or the line will tangle. If the fly and line are to your right (and you want to roll it to the left), the casting stroke must be made from the right side. If the fly is off to the left (and you want to cast to the right), make the stroke from the left side. Practice both ways. If you are casting with your right hand and want to bring the rod back over the left shoulder, reposition your stance so that the right side of your body and right foot are slightly forward. Be sure, however, that you keep your thumb behind the grip and your knuckles pointing toward the direction for the cast for best control. And, while not absolutely necessary, don't be afraid to practice casting with your left hand if you are right handed, and vice versa. It can come in handy, and it's easier than you think.

Bring the rod well back, as for a normal roll cast, except over the opposite shoulder. Keep the thumb behind the grip and the knuckles pointing toward the target for better control and accuracy.

Wait for the line to stop moving for just a second and begin the forward stroke.

Accelerate the forward stroke.

Stop the rod tip while it is moving out and away.

Follow the line to the water with the rod.

The same cast from
behind the caster.

Roll-Cast Pickup

Normally when executing a roll cast you simply let the line roll forward and straighten out over the water ahead of you. In other words, it serves as your forward cast to present the fly. However, the roll-cast pickup uses the roll cast to get the end of the line moving so you can execute a normal backcast/forward cast sequence. When you make the roll cast, watch the leader and fly. As soon as the fly leaves the water, make your normal backcast, followed by a forward cast.

A common fault when fishing a dry fly upstream is to strip in all the slack until you don't have enough line to make a good backcast. You will then have to make a series of false casts to work out the line you just stripped in. In situations like this, employ the roll-cast pickup. It is often the best way to pick up a dry fly, bass bug, or sinking line.

The roll-cast pickup is particularly suitable for changing directions when picking up wet flies. For example, suppose you cast up and across with the stream flowing from your left to your right. When the line straightens it is below you downstream to your right. Most fishermen will then make a series of false casts—back, forward, back, forward—while gradually rotating their body until they face up and across stream for their final cast. This is inefficiency in the extreme. Too much energy is used to accomplish a simple objective. Also, you risk catching a backcast in the bushes since each cast goes in a different plane. You will also have shaken the water from the fly, as you would do with a dry fly, so it will not sink readily. If at all possible, the longest your fly should be out of the water is for one backcast.

Instead, don't start with a backcast but with a roll cast. If your line is downstream, make a roll cast almost directly across. You will have already cut the distance to your final target in half. Now, with the back and forward casts you can place the fly up and across for another drift, never using more than one backcast. You may have to do the roll-cast pickup over the opposite shoulder (as described earlier). This is necessary if the above situation occurs and the stream is flowing right to left.

Begin as for a normal roll cast, rod tip well back. Wait just a moment for the line on the water to stop moving toward you.

Make the normal forward roll cast, high and away.

The loop forms.

The line unrolls, tight and flat.

The fly leaves the water as the loop approaches completion.

Just before the end of the loop straightens, slowly start your backcast motion.

Continue to accelerate.

Stop the rod as for a normal backcast by stabbing the
rod tip in the direction you want the line to go.

Wait, maintaining your position while the loop unrolls.

Just before the loop straightens completely, begin moving the rod forward.

As always, the final acceleration is made once the rod has
come past your face, into your peripheral vision.

Stop the rod, aiming about eye level.

Keep the rod pointed in the direction of the line's flow. After the line straightens and starts to fall, lower the rod with it to the water.

Mini Roll-Cast Pickup

To pick up a dry fly off the water as it floats toward you, employ a very abbreviated form of the roll-cast pickup. It's excellent for short-line situations.

Give a quick flick forward with the rod tip. A small loop will roll down the line.

Just as the fly lifts from the water. . . .

. . . make your normal backcast.

When you make the roll cast, with the line pinched by the index finger of the casting hand place your left hand, palm open, up along the rod at least half way to the stripping guide. As the rod strikes your outstretched palm, the line will jump quickly into a tight, sharp loop and go a few extra feet.

Cheat Roll Cast

Occasionally you may find that you need a few extra feet but can't manage to roll far enough without the line collapsing. Perhaps your technique needs some work or perhaps it's just beyond your range. Often you just don't have room to make the full stroke. For want of a better term I call the solution the "cheat roll cast." Simply make a normal roll cast but run the rod into the open palm of your left hand. The abrupt stop will make the line jump into a tight roll and usually get a few extra feet. It isn't pretty but it works. I use it a lot in tight quarters where my rod motion is restricted.

Freeing a Snag

If your fly hangs on a log, you may free it if you can pull from the opposite direction. Unless the hook is embedded deeply, simply feed out some extra line and make a roll cast. As soon as the unrolling line goes beyond the obstacle and while it is still in the air, make a quick backcast. Most often, the fly will come clear. This is really nothing more than another application of the roll-cast pickup. Check your fly and hook and continue fishing.

The fly is hooked on the end of the branch. Make the normal forward roll cast. When the line rolls past the log, it will often pull the fly loose from the opposite direction. When the fly pops into the air, make the normal backcast and forward cast.

Extended Roll for Distance

Actually this is not a true roll cast but a hybrid, a combination of a roll/forward stroke, preceded by a weak backcast. Some of the load comes from the line behind you and the rest from the line on the water in front of you. Weakly throw a loop of line to the rear, which serves as a backcast. Try to limit the line on the water in front of you to no more than about two rod lengths. Just as the line falls and touches the water, make your forward stroke. It takes a little practice to time the start of the forward cast just right, but when backcast room is limited and you must extend extra line on the forward cast, this is an ideal technique.

Instead of sliding the line back on the water as for a normal roll cast, lift it weakly off the water.

Throw it low
behind you.

The line starts
to fall to the water
to the rear.

Start your forward cast just as the line touches the water.

Make a normal forward cast. Speed up. . . .

. . . and stop. . . .

. . . aiming high
and away.

Follow the line's
flight with the rod.

Notice that the line
exits the tip-top
straight away, not
going downward.

4

Distance

Increased distance is something for which all fly casters should strive. "Long casts have no disadvantages." I highlighted this sentence when I first read it in Lefty Kreh's *Fly Fishing in Salt Water*. This doesn't, of course, mean that you should always cast long or that a long cast is always better than a short cast. What it does mean is that the ability to cast long, to get the fly there when it has to be there, is without disadvantage.

Keep in mind too that distance is a relative term, not an absolute measurement in terms of inches and feet. Under really adverse conditions, a forty-foot cast may be nearly impossible, and we can rightly call it a long cast. Yet under ideal conditions, with clear backcast room, little wind, and so forth, twice that distance might be considered only moderate. Furthermore, to make some of the fishing casts to be discussed later, like slack-line and hook casts, you must sometimes make a potential seventy-five-foot cast to get to a target fifty feet away, since all the energy isn't used in merely straightening the line. So what we call "long" may vary.

Probably more fishermen are concerned about their inability to cast longer distances with control and accuracy than they are about any other aspect of casting. This is ironic, since the principles behind longer casts are precisely the same as those employed in making that twenty-footer on a small stream. The caster who claims to be able to cast at short range but who can't make long casts really isn't casting well at any range. Not only is he unable to cope with the demands of large salmon rivers or tarpon flats, he probably can't toss large bugs, weighted flies, make hook and slack-line casts, aerial mends, cope with wind, or do other things the proficient caster can.

Often when fly fishers claim, "I only fish small waters," "Long casts aren't necessary," or "Most fish are caught within forty feet," there is a sad corollary to their comments: They restrict themselves to small waters because they haven't the ability to cope with the problems of longer casts, larger flies, obstacles, and wind. They are trying to justify their limited skills. They can enjoy exciting sport from a hundred species, but they must first determine to improve their technique. If you can only cast fifty feet under ideal conditions, your ability to perform will be inadequate in many fishing situations. Guides in Florida, Montana, and other popular fishing locales often complain of their clients' inability to cast under adverse conditions or with heavy tackle. When you consider wind, air-resistant flies, obstructions, a rocking boat, or deep wading, your best efforts may only net you twenty-five or thirty feet, and then only with a lot of work. As a rule of thumb you should be striving for the ability to throw eighty- to one hundred-foot casts easily and comfortably, standing on the lawn, with a standard weight-forward outfit.

If you can make smooth, effortless longer casts, your shorter casts will be that much easier too. I have heard other critics claim that you can't set the hook at one hundred feet or so with a fly rod. I disagree. If the fish is one hundred feet away you haven't any choice, and surf casters regularly hook fish at well over one hundred yards using monofilament line with far more stretch than any fly line.

I can sum up distance casting in terms of two basic notions: Make the casting stroke much longer and the loop much tighter. Remember, the longer the cast, the farther you must move the rod. By moving the rod farther (not necessarily harder), you can get the rod more deeply loaded, get the line straighter before casting it, and smooth out your stroke, all without hard, forceful motions or exceptional coordination and timing.

As for the second part, remember that a tight loop travels faster, farther, straighter. It is often claimed that a wide loop provides too much wind resistance to travel forward efficiently, but wind resistance is negligible. The really critical point is that the energy in a wide loop is directed off at tangents by the front of the unrolling line. Much of that energy is dissipated in directions other than that in which we want the line to go; hence we work harder but get indifferent results for our effort. Most fly fishermen are amazed at how effortlessly a good caster can throw ninety feet of line. First note the size of his loop and then how far he moves the rod (or how hard he casts if he doesn't).

Don't merely cast harder to cast farther. That is the only option you will have if you insist upon casting within a given range, say ten o'clock to one o'clock or so. On the other hand, if you continually lengthen the backcast and forward cast arcs, basic physics assures that you can make eighty-foot casts with about the same effort that you used for thirty-footers. Earlier I emphasized varying the stopping position of the backcast for various length casts and suggested turning the hand to the side before beginning longer casts. It will be easier to make your backcast a bit off to the side and lower as well as to reach your arm well back.

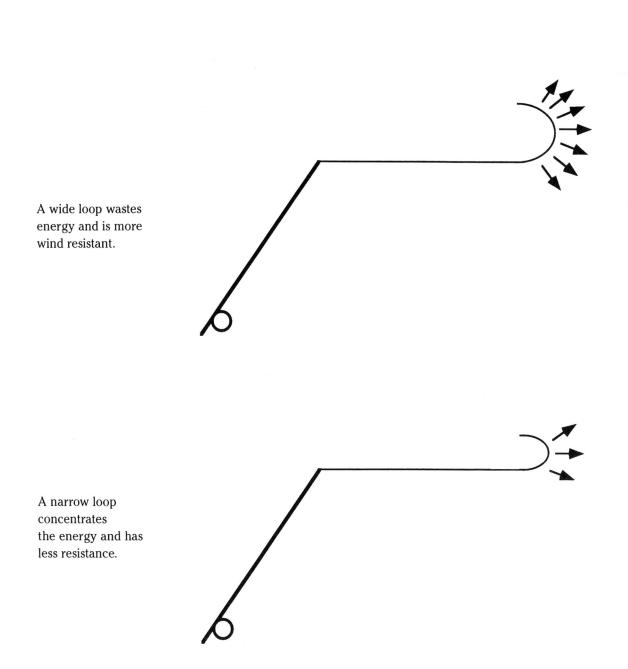

A wide loop wastes
energy and is more
wind resistant.

A narrow loop
concentrates
the energy and has
less resistance.

Long-Line Pickup

Under many fishing conditions you will find it easier to make longer casts if you don't retrieve so much line and you pick up more line off the water. Since you already have more line in the air, you have less line to shoot.

Another important point to mention: When striving for greater distance, whether throwing a ball, shooting an arrow, or casting a fly, you need elevation and so must aim higher. You wouldn't try to throw a baseball from center field to home plate with the same short motion needed to toss the ball ten feet. You would bring your arm well back and throw in an upward direction. It sounds heretical, but you should make the lowest backcast that conditions allow, particularly when making longer casts.

This is another reason so many people who use a short, restricted stroke have difficulty when attempting more distance. They have difficulty aiming higher, since all their motion tends to go in a downward direction. Now to aim higher you must stop sooner, which actually means you are using a shorter stroke, hence you must cast harder. You also need more critical timing. If you are going to shorten the stroke in front of you, make the stroke behind you longer—it's common sense and good physics.

The left hand also becomes more important when making longer casts. Understanding the task of the left hand is vital to shooting and controlling line and making hauls—a useful element of longer casts. If your left hand doesn't work properly on longer casts, it probably isn't working properly at shorter distances either. The effects just aren't so pronounced. Incidentally, a left hand that doesn't work effectively will hurt your casting more than one that isn't used at all.

Shooting Line

As your casting becomes more efficient you will be able to shoot more line, thus adding to the line you have outside the rod tip when you make the cast. Here's how you can get there. Once you have become accustomed to keeping your hands about the same distance apart throughout a normal, short to moderate cast, try shooting some line: As the right hand completes the casting stroke, just as it makes the final speed-up and stops, simply open the fingers of the left hand and release the line. Don't pull, push, or anything else—just let go of the line. Depending on how well you coordinate the release with the stop of the right hand, a certain amount of line laying at your feet will shoot out through the guides. Practice until you consistently release the line and shoot at least ten or fifteen feet of extra line. You can let extra line slip out on the backcast in the same way: When you stop the rod, let a few feet of line slip through the fingers of your left hand and grasp it tight again, so that the backcast travels a little farther. If you shoot five feet on the backcast and fifteen feet on the forward cast, you will have already turned a thirty-foot cast into a fifty-footer.

Keeping the rod tip low, lean forward, reach out, and grasp the line with your left hand close to the stripping guide.

Keep your line hand close to the stripping guide while raising the rod for the backcast.

Continue to accelerate the rod as . . .

. . . you start to
straighten your body.

Just as the end of
the line starts to leave
the water . . .

. . . you should be
approaching
maximum
acceleration.

Stab the rod to the
rear and stop, making
certain the rod hand
is moving slightly
upward when it stops.

No drift is needed.
The rod and arm are
already positioned
to make the forward
cast.

Wait while the
line . . .

. . . unrolls to the rear.

Before the line straightens completely (the loop will look like a J or a candy cane), slowly start moving the rod hand forward and continue to speed up.

Just about the time the hand comes into your peripheral vision, you should be nearing maximum acceleration.

Stop the rod tip pointing the direction you want the line to go.

Allow the forward cast to unroll . . .

. . . until it straightens in the air.

Follow the line as it
falls with the rod.

Continue lowering the
rod to fishing position.

The Double Haul

The next step to adding distance is learning to haul. Hauling is a misunderstood and hence misused technique. Throughout this text I have talked about the rapid speed-up and stop that comes at the end of the casting stroke, whether it is a backcast or forward cast. When you haul, you simply add a short, quick pull on the line with the left (line) hand, precisely at the same time as the right (rod) hand makes its final speed-up. Essentially, the hands pull apart at this point. This motion increases the line's speed as well as the load on the rod tip so that it generates higher speed when it straightens.

If you haul only when you make the backcast or only when you make the forward cast, it is dubbed a single haul. If you haul on both casts (remember, the back and forward casts are two separate casts), it is known as a double haul. It is not reserved only for long casts. Good casters apply short hauls instinctively even when casting short and moderate distances. The double haul simply makes any cast easier, and that is what this book is all about—finding ways to use as little effort as possible for *any* cast.

You needn't make long, exaggerated pulls with the left hand. Actually, once you realize that only the left-hand pull that occurs during the right-hand final speed-up really effectively translates into a benefit, you will realize that all the long pulling and stretching some casters go through is wasted motion. The short hauls recommended here will develop terrific line speed with incredibly little effort if you haul exactly as the right hand gets to the final acceleration.

A good way to learn to double haul is to practice it in parts on the grass then gradually put the parts together. When you make the backcast with the haul, let the line fall to the ground. Rehearse in your mind what you will do on the forward cast and then make the forward cast. Finally, when your muscles are accustomed to hauling in each direction, put them together into continuous back and forward casts.

I once had a student who only wanted to learn to double haul. When I pointed out that his basic casting needed a lot of work and that we should first talk about that, he walked away in a huff. The double haul is not some magic technique that will miraculously assure long casts. Quite the contrary; it is a modification of the basic cast, employing the left hand only momentarily. Too many casters camouflage poor technique with the double haul. They learn to cast fifty feet or so and then start pumping the line, pulling way down and up, huffing and puffing their way through the double haul. They are working far too hard. Usually they are mediocre casters who have developed a well-timed double haul. They aren't casting better, only throwing their mistakes farther.

To find out if your basic cast needs work, I first recommend that you put your line hand in your pocket or by your side. If you can't make a long cast using just one hand, your basic stroke should be improved or you will never get full benefit from the double haul . . . and it will never be easy.

The two hands are close together during the backcast.

As the right hand makes its short, rapid acceleration, the left hand simultaneously accelerates for a similar distance, pulling away from the right hand . . .

. . . then travels a short distance to return close to the reel and in line with the rod.

The right hand makes the forward cast and . . .

. . . just as it makes its short, rapid forward acceleration . . .

. . . the left hand again pulls down, just as in the backcast. The left hand releases the line precisely as the right hand stops the rod.

Using Shooting Tapers

Specialized fly lines known as shooting tapers (or shooting heads) are commonly employed when distance is a primary fishing concern. Essentially a shooting taper is the front thirty feet or so of a weight-forward line. To the rear is attached a running (or shooting) line of monofilament, braided monofilament, or very narrow fly line. This running line goes through the guides with less drag than an ordinary fly line so that extra distance is achieved. You pay a price for this advantage, however. Once cast, the shooting taper cannot be picked up until you strip it nearly all the way back to the rod. You also can't modify the cast in the air (which I'll discuss in the next chapter) once you have sent it on its way. It's sort of like casting a spinning lure. Finally, casting a shooting taper requires great attention to one detail.

When you cast a shooting taper, don't feed too much running line out past the rod tip when false casting. The distance from the tip-top to the back end of the shooting head is called the "overhang." Try to use only a few feet of overhang. If it becomes longer you get a hinging effect as the weak running line can't turn over the fly line properly. Note in the photographs what happens with a proper overhang and what happens when it becomes too long.

Allow no more than a few feet of overhang beyond the rod tip when you pick up to make your backcast.

With the proper length of overhang, a good loop will form on the forward cast . . .

. . . and continue to unroll toward the target as you shoot extra line.

With too much overhang, the shooting line will hinge and cause disastrous results as shown here.

Water Haul/Double Water Haul

Some fishing situations, in the ocean or deep, swift rivers for instance, call for very heavy sinking lines and flies. Such gear is difficult for most anglers to use, and not only because of the weight of the outfit. The problem lies in the fact that the sunken line offers tremendous resistance to the pickup. Even if you can muscle the line out of the water, when it comes free of the water resistance the rod, deeply bent and overloaded, will recoil and throw shock waves into the line. Consequently, many people find sinking lines uncomfortable to use.

The best way to deal with sinking lines, sink-tip lines, shooting tapers, and such, particularly when fishing heavy flies, is to employ a modified roll-cast pickup combined with a double haul called a "water haul." The point is to roll the heavy line onto the surface so that it can be picked up more easily while using the water to provide some resistance. Allowing for the heavier weight rod, line, and fly, the whole operation should be about as smooth and effortless as your normal pickup and cast with a floating line. Long, extended motions to the front and rear are the key.

When fishing extremely heavy lines and flies, the "double water haul" may be called for. This involves not only making the roll cast onto the water but also letting the backcast fall to the water for an instant to keep the line and fly under control and gain added load from the surface tension when you make the forward cast.

Some Final Notes on Improving Distance

Attention to some seemingly minor details can make casting easier. While these are not strictly casting pointers, I feel that anything that wastes any of the energy, however little, in a cast should be remedied. These can turn twenty-foot casts into twenty-five-foot casts or sixty-foot casts into seventy-five-foot casts.

Always stretch the line and leader before fishing. The line's "memory" retains the coils it got from being stored on the reel. The line will not perform at its best unless it has been straightened.

Dirty fly lines drag through the guides and knock distance from all casts, even short ones. You must therefore cast just a little harder to make up for the lost energy, so get into the habit of cleaning your lines regularly. There are many excellent cleaners and dressings on the market.

Small guides, both stripping guides on the butt and snake guides above, restrict the flow of the line, again making you work harder. Make sure that your stripping guide is at least twelve millimeters in diameter for lighter lines (2- to 6-weight), sixteen millimeters or larger for heavier lines. Finally, inspect and clean the guides regularly. Dirt can restrict line flow, and grooves, especially in the tip-top, can inhibit casting and destroy the finish on a fly line in short order.

Bring the rod back to the starting position for a roll cast.

Make a roll cast, stroking the rod forward.

Allow it to roll out a few feet above the water.

As the line straightens out and begins to fall, follow it down, lowering the rod tip and reaching the rod and hands well forward.

Just as the line touches the water, begin raising the rod.

Make a normal pickup.

Make your backcast (followed by a regular forward cast, if desired).

This is an optional move. Instead of making a regular forward cast, reach the rod and hands well to the rear, allowing the backcast to touch down briefly behind you.

Make the forward cast off the water; this supplies extra load and helps control the heavy line and fly.

Aim your forward cast high.

5

Practical Fishing Casts I

The casts discussed in this chapter have one thing in common: They all involve some variation of one of the Four Principles done during the execution of the cast. A particular element such as the speed or angle has been adjusted to make the cast. Other useful casts, which will be covered in the next chapter, involve line manipulations after the casting stroke has been completed. This, it seems to me, is the most natural way to divide the many useful fishing presentations.

Wind From the Right

A wind coming directly against the casting arm (from the right in the case of a right-handed caster) presents obvious difficulties. There are several ways of dealing with it. Casting with the left hand is one of the first things to consider. Making the backcast over the left shoulder (discussed in chapter 2) is another option. Here is a very straightforward solution for severe conditions.

Start your pickup to
the side, with the rod
tip low.

Continue accelerating
your backcast, rod
parallel to the water.
This keeps the line
well clear of you on
the backcast.

Continue to
accelerate.

When the rod hand gets about perpendicular to the direction of the cast and the whole line is moving smoothly toward you, begin the final acceleration of the cast. With the rod so low you may not be able to get the whole line off the water. The end of the fly line must be moving before you make the final acceleration.

Continue to speed up and stop the rod by stabbing it straight back.

Wait for the line to unroll.

Just before the line completely straightens, slowly start moving the rod forward, directly over your head. Remember that a strong wind from the right will push the line to the left so that the line will be passing the caster safely on that side.

On the forward cast, just as the rod hand comes into your peripheral vision, the final acceleration begins.

The cast finishes with the rod tip moving straight ahead and a few feet over the water.

Keep the rod pointed in the direction of the line flow while the loop unrolls.

As the line begins to fall . . .

. . . follow it with the rod tip until you are back in fishing position.

Barnegat Bay Cast

If the wind is particularly strong and persistent, try the Barnegat Bay cast. I know a number of saltwater casters who use it regularly along the New Jersey surf in the vicinity of Barnegat Bay, where a persistent and frustrating southeast wind blows right up the beach much of the season, causing a problem for right-handers. This technique has been used by many fly casters in many places for a long time, and I am certain it has other names. Really it amounts to nothing more than turning your back to the wind and letting your backcast fall to the water. If you recognize that the forward and backcasts are the same except for traveling in different directions, you will have no trouble with this one.

With your back to the wind, make a false cast away from the target. Before the cast straightens out, go into a normal backcast.

Stab the backcast
high and away from
you. Allow the line
to straighten out and
fall to the water.

You can also turn
your hand so that
you are effectively
making a forward
cast. This technique
is good when
accuracy is a factor.

Start as for a normal
pickup but . . .

. . . make a horizontal backcast, low
and to the side.

Keeping the rod parallel to the water, stop the final acceleration by stabbing the rod straight back.

Reach well back. The line should be very low, just above the water. It may even touch briefly, but this won't hurt the cast.

Before the line straightens completely, start your forward cast.

Your final acceleration should begin just as the rod hand comes into your peripheral vision. Aim high.

Finish with the rod tip stopping in an upward direction.

By starting well back and low, and by using long strokes, you can cast high so that the line travels safely well above you. The following wind helps carry the line even farther forward.

Wind From the Rear

Strangely enough, a following wind often causes more difficulty than a head wind or crosswind. This is particularly so if you insist upon stopping your backcast high at the traditional twelve o'clock or one o'clock position.

Here is one effective way to defeat the wind that hampers your backcast while utilizing it to make your forward cast.

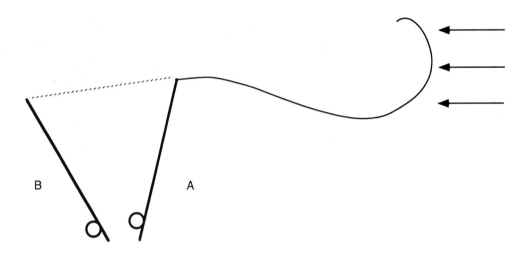

If you stop your backcast at one o'clock and a strong wind from the rear pushes it back toward you, creating slack in the loop, you will waste nearly all your forward travel just pulling slack line.

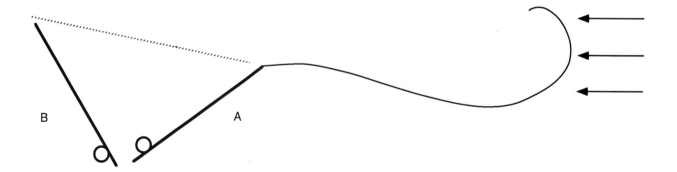

Stop the rod well back. Even if the wind interferes with the backcast and some of the motion will be used to eliminate slack, you can still load the rod for a forward cast.

If you cast high when the line straightens, a wind in your face will push the line back toward you.

Wind From the Front

Dealing with a head wind involves recognition of the fact that as long as line is unrolling, it will be moving forward, and it only starts to collapse once it has straightened.

Since the wind can only push the line back toward the caster after it has straightened and is falling to the water, make certain that when the line finishes unrolling it is mere inches above the surface, thus eliminating the opportunity for the wind to interfere. Remember also that a tighter loop will travel farther and faster. I am amazed at how many casters—even instructors—recommend driving the rod tip down hard toward the water. The loop this technique gives looks something like this and should be avoided:

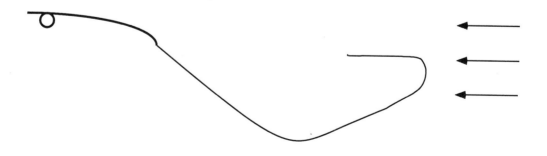

Don't cast down hard toward the water to fight a head wind. The belly in the loop shows that much of the energy in this cast is being wasted. Compare this curve to the symmetrical loop in the photograph of the recommended wind cast.

This cast, going by a variety of names, is highly inefficient because so much of the energy is driven down instead of ahead. One of the reasons you must drive the rod so hard is to make up for wasted energy. The loop may be wide or narrow but should always be symmetrical; if it's shaped otherwise it's a sure sign of using too much energy. Here's how to make a far more energy-efficient cast requiring less effort and developing incredible line speed.

Just before the backcast straightens, start your forward cast as you normally would, with a smooth continuous increase in speed.

As you make the final acceleration, squat down a bit. Raise the elbow of your casting arm so that your forearm is parallel to the water just as you start the final acceleration.

Stop the rod by stabbing your whole arm straight ahead. Don't stroke down toward the water. Notice that the rod tip finishes nearly parallel to the water.

By finishing straight ahead you eliminate guide friction and don't waste energy by driving the line down toward the water.

When executed properly, the loop is a very tight V and travels extemely fast.

Reverse or Galway Cast

Wind isn't the only obstacle to comfortable fishing. Along many trout streams bushes and trees are an ever-present frustration to our backcasts. Here's a cast I also use often when floating smallmouth streams and when snook fishing in narrow mangrove creeks. Since most people can make a more accurate forward cast than backcast, simply employ two forward casts.

Hold the rod tip low, pointed straight down the line. Before starting, turn the rod hand so that the reel and guides are facing up with the thumb now on the bottom of the grip.

Continue raising the rod as for a normal backcast (except that the hand is turned), all the while increasing the speed of the rod.

When the end of the
fly line starts to
leave the water, you
should start the
short final
acceleration.

Speed up and stop
the tip in the
direction you want
the line to go.

You actually are
making a forward
cast to the rear,
aiming at the
opening in the trees
or to the left or
right of the obstacle.

Keep the rod pointed
in the direction
of the line's flight.

Just before the line
straightens out fully,
turn back toward
your target.

Make a normal
forward cast, starting
slowly and
continuing to
increase in speed.

The final
acceleration begins
as the rod comes
into your peripheral
vision.

As always, finish the
cast with the tip-top
moving exactly the
direction you want
the line to travel.

As the line falls,
follow it to the water
with the rod tip.
You are now back in
fishing position.

Hook and Curve Casts

Among the most useful of all fishing casts is the hook cast. Don't confuse this with the reach cast. In the true hook cast, the line travels out in front of the caster, but the last few feet of line and the leader hook sharply around to the right or left and land on the water up to ninety degrees to the general direction of the cast. This cast has many useful applications, and the experienced fly fisher uses it, or at least should use it, regularly.

The advantage of being able to cast around rocks, stumps, brush piles, and other obstructions is obvious, but there are many other routine situations in which the hook cast can spell the difference between success and failure. Consider this situation: You are floating downriver in a raft, driftboat, or canoe casting toward the bank with a dry fly or popper. As soon as the fly lands, the faster water near your boat drags the fly from the slower water against the bank, giving only a momentary opportunity for a fish to get a look at it. You can solve the problem easily by casting toward the shore and having the line hook sharply downstream. The line closer to the caster, since it lands upstream, can sweep along in the faster current without dragging the last few feet of line, leader, and fly. The hook cast can make the difference between a drag-free float of just a few inches or many feet and is much more effective than any slack-line cast in this situation.

Another scenario: You cast your streamer toward a grassy bank across the stream. If you've thrown in a straight line, when you start to retrieve you begin pulling the fly away from the bank immediately, giving any fish over there only a fleeting glimpse of your offering. If you cast toward the bank and have the last few feet of line and leader hook sharply so that they land parallel to the bank, either up- or downstream, when you start to retrieve the fly travels right along the bank for the first five or ten feet before it turns and starts moving toward you. This keeps the fly in the fish's vicinity longer. Similarly, on a pond you can throw around a patch of lily pads and make your bass bug swim to the right or left rather than simply straight back toward you. Once you learn to throw hooks, you'll wonder how you ever fished without them.

Hook to the Left

Here's how to make the basic hook cast. Let's assume we are casting right-handed and want to throw a hook around to the left. The principle with which we are most concerned here is the fourth, namely that the line will go in the direction the tip is moving when it stops. Simply hold the rod well off the vertical position, to the side. Cast a little harder than normal and stop the rod very smartly. You can think "push the thumb to the left" or "turn the knuckles to the left" as long as you make the motion brief and the tip finishes with a quick curve to the left (staying the same distance above the water, not moving downward). The line will go forward and snap around sharply to the left and fall to the water in that configuration. The left hook (occasionally called a "positive" hook) is one of the easiest casts to make and one of the most useful.

Make the cast as usual, but when you speed up and stop at the end of the forward stroke, turn the hand sharply (as shown in the close-up photos following). The line will travel forward . . .

. . . hook around sharply to the left . . .

. . . and land behind the obstacle.

These photos show
the movement of the
casting hand to
make a hook to the
left. When making
the forward cast,
instead of stopping
the rod straight
ahead turn the hand
sharply to the left as
you make the final
acceleration and
stop—not before
or after. This will
turn the tip-top
sharply to the left,
and of course
the line will do the
same.

Here is a left hook shown from above. Note that you
can make the line hook up to ninety degrees.

Distance and accuracy with the hook cast depend on several variables, especially how briefly you make the final acceleration and how far forward you bring the rod before stopping—the farther back you stop the rod, the farther out the hook will occur. If you manage to perform the basic hook, practice until you can make it with reasonable accuracy and consistency at different distances by varying your stroke length. You will be amazed at just how much control you can develop.

Hook to the Right

If you want the line to hook to the right, you must make the tip finish in a tight curve going that direction. By far the simplest way is to follow the above instructions, except cast with your left hand. It is really much simpler than you think. You can also use the right hand but cast across your body with the rod pointing out to the left. Finally, you can cast with the rod in an essentially normal position, but when you come forward, cast a little harder and turn your hand sharply out to the right as you speed-up and stop. (This is the opposite of the left hook above, although it is a little more difficult for most people to turn the hand that direction.) This will cause the line to go forward and kick around sharply to the right. Remember, you can't stop and then turn your hand. The line will keep going straight if you stop the rod movement in that direction.

A number of older texts recommend simply doing a greatly underpowered horizontal cast so that a sloppy loop falls on the water with a curve to the right—sometimes called a "negative" hook cast since it never completes itself. This is a highly imprecise maneuver. I have never seen anyone execute it with any degree of consistency or accuracy. Furthermore, you can't cast around obstructions with it since the loop is leading and the fly simply flops behind on the water.

Make a normal backcast, but finish the forward cast with a brief speed-up and stop while turning the hand sharply to the right. (See close-up photos of hand position.) Here the line is just starting to turn back to the right.

The fly and leader have hooked ninety degrees to the right and landed behind the bush.

Similar to the hook to the left, except that here the hand directs the rod to the right.

Curve Cast

Throwing a curve is simple, for it is essentially a less emphatic hook. Keep the rod more vertical, and as you complete the forward stroke, push your thumb slightly to the left or right, instead of straight ahead. The tip of the rod will finish in a similar direction, causing the line to follow a similar course and fall to the water in a slight curve.

The curve cast. Here the speed-up and stop was made with the hand turning less sharply and the thumb pushing the grip slightly to the left, resulting in the line moving in a more curved path.

Up-Hook Cast

Here is a favorite variation on this theme. In essence it is a hook upward, so I simply call it the up-hook cast. Picture the basic left hook on its side. Throw a horizontal cast but instead of stopping the rod straight in front of you, make the final acceleration and stop by sharply turning the hand up and immediately lowering the tip back down to a level position. The line on this cast goes forward, turns up, and drops back to the water with curves of slack line, all out at the front end of the cast. With this cast you can float a dry fly longer because there is a lot of slack near the end of the line and in the leader. You can put a heavy line on the water with less disturbance, since all the energy of the cast is expended upward and the line merely settles back. And you can keep your cast low to the water and not spook fish as readily as you might with a line eight or ten feet in the air. Lefty Kreh first came up with this cast when confronted by spooky fish on the bonefish flats. It's a great one. To emphasize the motion, I show the cast here done especially high.

Make a horizontal backcast.

Make a horizontal forward cast, but make the final speed-up and stop with the hand, and hence the rod tip, turning sharply upward. This is performed like the hook to the left except that you turn your knuckles upward instead of to the left.

Immediately upon stopping the rod, lower the tip.

The line will fall to the water with a lot of slack in the forward portion of the line and the leader.

Here is a close-up look at this useful cast. Make the back and forward casts in a horizontal plane.

The final part of the forward stroke is made with a sharp upturn of the hand. The thumb directs the rod sharply upward. (Here the motion is slightly exaggerated for clarity.)

Immediately drop the rod tip back down toward the water.

Steeple Cast

When obstructions prevent your making a backcast to the rear or even to the side, use the steeple cast. Your aim is to make the backcast to go nearly straight up. The cast is shown here first as it is typically done and then in what I consider a more efficient method. The improved technique represents another example of always keeping the Four Principles in mind; specifically, in this case, the line *must* go the direction the tip was moving when it stopped.

The steeple cast. Even if you make a very high backcast . . .

. . . the line is still traveling rearward toward the obstacle, as the line coming from the rod tip shows.

For an improved steeple cast, turn the rod upside down, guides and reel facing upward.

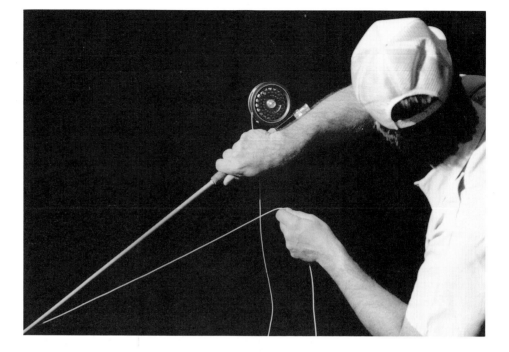

Now make the high backcast, with the thumb pushing from underneath.

With this method you can stop the rod tip while it is traveling in a more vertical path. You can see that the line is climbing almost vertically. Turn your hand and make a normal forward cast.

Change of Direction on the Backcast

Suppose you have cast up and across a stream and your line has floated downstream until it is directly below you. Now you wish to repeat the same drift. (This situation was described when discussing the roll-cast pickup. Use this alternative if the cast to be made is not too long.) Don't waste motion with a series of back and forward casts while gradually rotating your body back to the direction of the final cast. Just remember that every cast is a matter of getting the end of the line moving, accelerating, and stopping in the direction you want the line to go. Just use the water resistance to help load the rod and curve the backcast stroke.

The current from left to right is pulling against the line, and you want to recast directly across the stream.

Start drawing the rod upstream with the tip nearly touching the water.

Keep bringing
the rod around,
gradually
accelerating.

When the rod is
lined up with the
target . . .

. . . make your
backcast directly to
the rear. The water's
resistance has
helped load the rod.

When the line
is nearly straight
behind you . . .

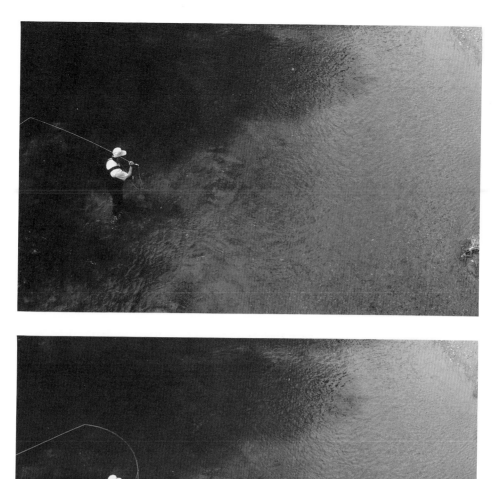

. . . make your
normal forward cast.

Notice no false casts
and only one
backcast were used
to change the angle
of the cast ninety
degrees or more.

Change of Direction on the Forward Cast

The cast above assumes you have room for a backcast behind you. If you lack space, make the backcast in whichever direction you have room and curve the stroke of the forward cast. You can easily make a forward cast ninety degrees to the direction of travel of the back cast.

With no room to the rear, make your
backcast off to your right.

The backcast here is at a right angle to the direction you want to cast.

Just before the line straightens completely, start bringing the rod tip around to the rear.

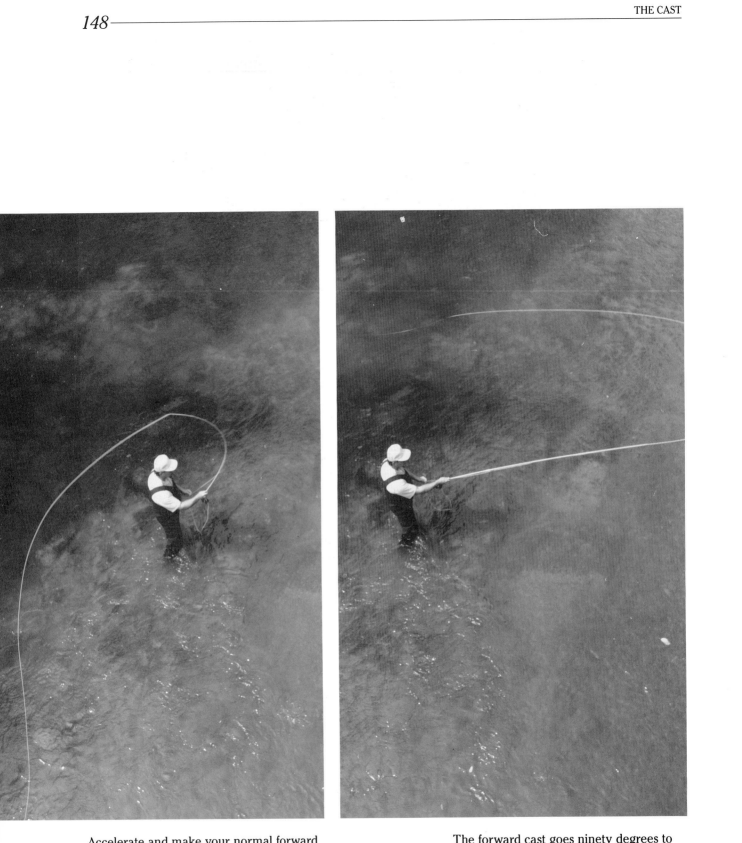

Accelerate and make your normal forward cast, directly across the stream.

The forward cast goes ninety degrees to the direction of the backcast, with no false casts.

The tuck cast, shown here at a high angle to emphasize the tuck. Make your forward cast harder than necessary, with a very abrupt stop. Some casters give a slight pull back when they stop the rod; the natural recoil of the rod will supply some of the same motion.

When the heavy fly straightens out the line and leader, it will bounce back and down toward the stream.

Tuck Cast

Often on a trout stream it's desirable to have a nymph or other fly sink quickly and on a slack line while it is coming downstream toward you. If you make a cast upstream so that the line and leader roll out straight ahead, the floating line will tether the leader and fly and prevent them from sinking. The line may also drag the fly downstream instead of letting it drift drag-free underwater. The tuck cast was designed for such situations. It causes the fly to enter the water with force so that it gets deep fast, yet creates slack so that it can sink freely. As with most of the casts described here, the tuck has many subtle variations. Learn the basic cast and experiment.

The fly will continue to come down at an angle, "tucking" itself under the line.

The fly enters the water with high velocity to get down fast.

The slack line falls to the surface, allowing the fly greater freedom to sink.

A horizontal cast is aimed about fifteen feet in front of the target area, with just enough force so that the fly skips on the surface and continues back under the obstruction.

Grasshopper or Skip Cast

Casting under branches and logs can present problems. Since the line will follow the direction of the rod tip, even a slight miscalculation (a subtle upturn of the hand at the conclusion of the cast) can make the line go forward, then rise up at the very end so that the fly rises and catches the branches. Everyone has at one time skipped a stone across the water. Do the same thing with your fly. Make a horizontal cast, aiming very slightly downward at a point ten or fifteen feet in front of the target area so that the fly briefly touches the water and then skips or bounces under the obstacle. The instant the fly touches the water it cancels any tendency to turn upward at the end, even if your hand did.

Catching the Line

Whether you want to clear grass from your fly, check the point, or change the fly, there is no need to strip or reel in all your line, yet anglers do this regularly. When ready to go again, they must work out all the line again before casting. Here's a quick and handy technique experienced fly casters use often.

Make a weak backcast directly overhead.

Bring the rod well back.

Reach your left hand
forward, palm open.

Let the end of the
line or, preferably,
the leader, fall
between your thumb
and index finger.

Grasp the leader
with the left hand . . .

. . . and instantly
make a weak
forward cast . . .

. . . so that the line
falls to the water
ahead of you. After
checking the fly,
roll-cast the line
forward out of your
hand.

6

Practical Fishing Casts II

In the casts discussed here, the basic casting stroke is first completed and only then is the line manipulated or altered to effect a desired result. The additional maneuvers take place after you have stopped the rod.

Reach Cast

To cast your line to the other side of the current and avoid drag as the fly floats downstream, use a reach cast. Simply make a normal cast and once the line is on its way, point and lower the rod (all the while letting line slip through your left hand) so that it points upstream by the time the line falls to the water. You can now follow the drift of the fly twice as long as if you finished with the rod pointing toward the target.

Here's another common situation calling for the reach cast. A trout is feeding twenty-five feet directly upstream. You can place your fly five or ten feet above the fish, but the line will drift right over it and spook it. If you can't move to the side and cast at an angle, the reach cast will achieve the same effect. Make your normal cast but immediately after you stop the rod, make the reach to the right or left. Remember, don't hold the line taut in your line hand—just let it slide over your fingers or palm. The fly can now drift straight down over the fish while the leader and line will float down off to one side.

The reach cast.
Make a normal
forward cast.

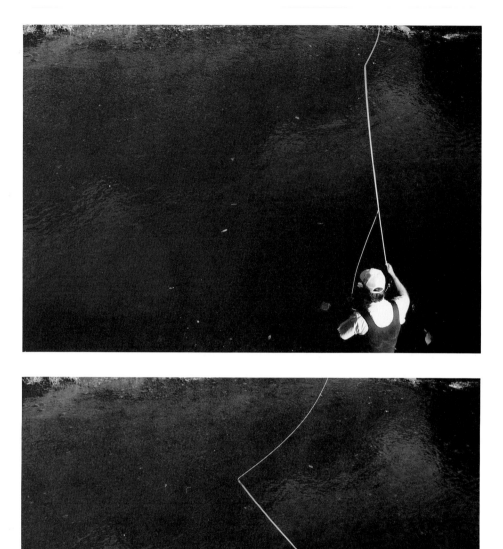

As the line is
unrolling, move
the rod to the
upstream side . . .

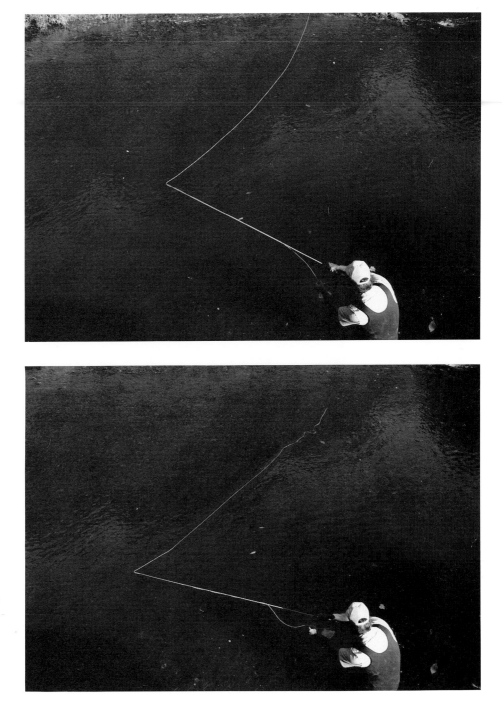

. . . lowering the
rod until . . .

. . . the tip is just
above the water as
the line lands. You
must feed line
through the fingers
of the left hand
during the reach or
the line will
straighten and be
pulled back from the
target.

This sequence shows the reach to the right, casting from the opposite side of the stream.

Slack-Line Casts

Many fishing situations call for the angler to present the fly so that there is slack in the line to prevent or forestall drag. Drag occurs when the line or leader pulls on the fly and makes it travel downstream faster than the current. A number of casts have been devised for this purpose. Following are some of the more useful ones.

Mending Line

Often you will want the fly to float or drift with no interference from the line or leader; when there isn't any slack, the line pulls against the fly and usually makes it behave most unnaturally. If it is a floating fly it may very well get pulled under. Mending is the traditional method for increasing the drag-free drift of a fly, dry or wet. Designing your leader so that it creates slack when it falls is important too, but here we are concerned only with casting.

After the line is on the water and starting to drift, flip the rod tip in the direction you want to place the mend. For example, normally if the current is flowing from your left to your right and the current closer to you is flowing faster than that where the fly is, flip the rod tip in a semicircular motion upstream, to the left, but just hard enough so that a belly of line develops and falls to the water without disturbing the leader and fly.

If you are casting out over slow water into faster water, the line farthest from you will drift faster than the line closest to you. In this case, mend your line downstream to extend your float.

The faster current in the center of the stream bellies the line and threatens to drag the fly downstream.

To compensate, starting with the rod tip close to the water, flip the rod tip upstream in a semicircular arc.

Try to mend only the belly of the line without moving the fly or pulling the slack out of the leader.

The bellied line is now upstream.

The fly can continue its drift in the slower water while the slack line floats along in the faster current.

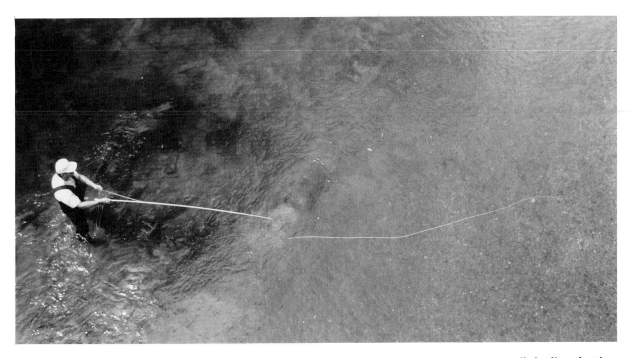

An overhead view of the mend. As the fast current threatens to pull the line that is closer to the angler downstream ahead of the fly . . .

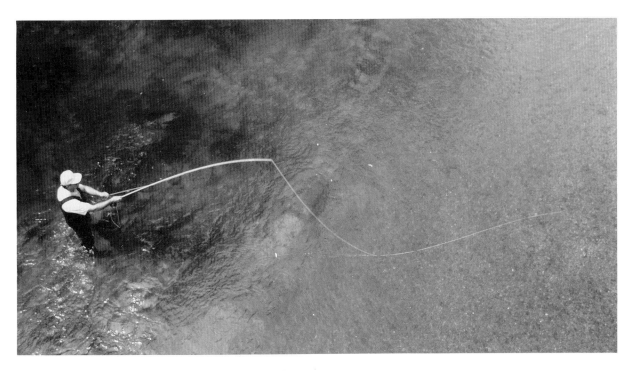

. . . raise the tip up and over . . .

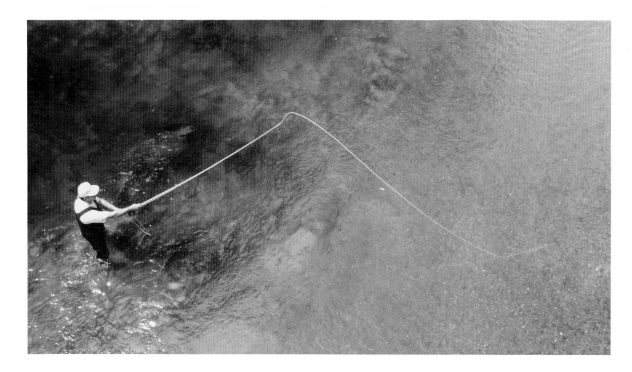

. . . in a circular arc . . .

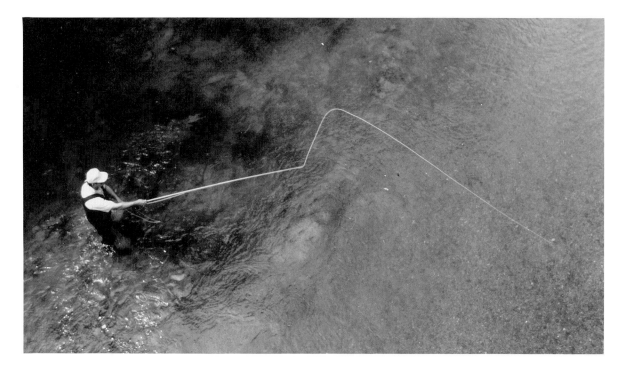

. . . throwing the slack line upstream.

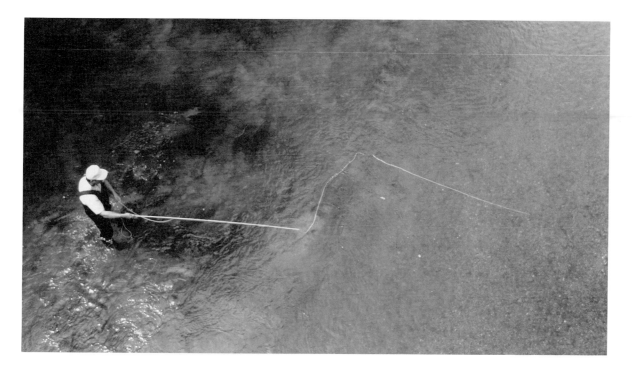

The fly floats without drag in the slower water to the far right of the photo . . .

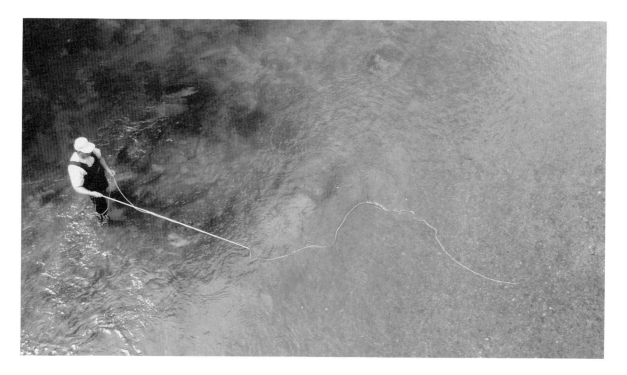

. . . while the slack line closer to the angler picks up speed.

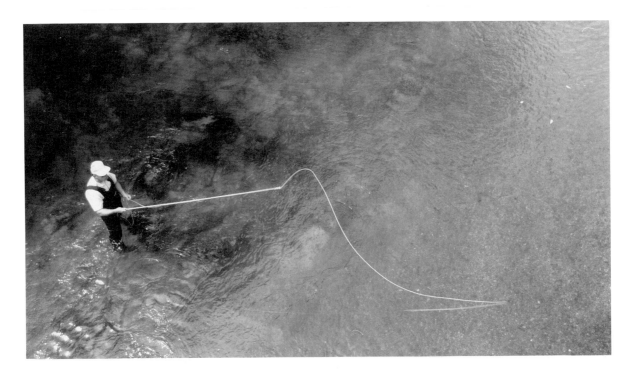

You can repeat the maneuver . . .

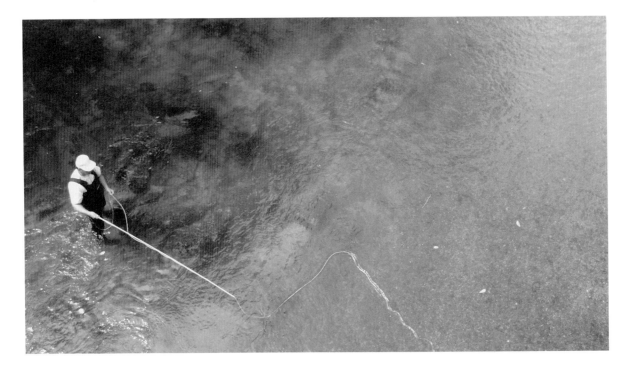

. . . to get even longer drag-free floats.

Aerial Mends

Mending line on the water is a basic and useful technique, but it has its shortcomings. Remember, it is important that you have some slack line or leader ahead of the fly to prevent drag. Often when mending line on the water you will pull the slack *out* of the line and shorten the length of your drag-free float. And once the line is on the water, you can only mend the line closest to the rod tip; you can't mend the line forty or fifty feet away without disturbing the line closest to you. If you simply remember that the line will continue moving in the direction you stopped the rod and realize you have time while waiting for the line to extend itself and fall to the water, you can make some truly impressive casts (and catch more fish).

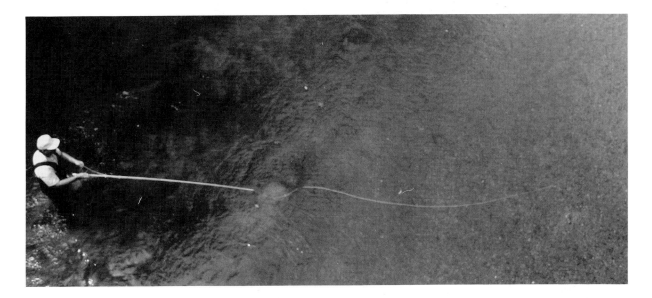

After you stop the rod on the forward cast and while the line is still in the air, quickly shake the tip back and forth once to the upstream direction.

Once you have made the cast and released the line in your left hand, shake the rod sharply once, out to the side and back again. A sharp curve will develop in the line to the side you shook the rod and run forward toward the end of the line. The line will fall to the water with the mend already in it. With practice you can make this mend as large as you want and place it at any point in the line and to either side. For example, let's say you want the mend to the right and out toward the very end of the line. After you stop the rod on your forward cast, immediately snap it smartly to the right and back again. You will see a single large curve form, run down the line, and fall to the water. If you want to make the mend larger simply shake the rod harder. To make the mend drop to the water closer to you, wait a second or so after you have stopped the rod and then shake it; the mend won't travel as far down the line. If you wait longer still before shaking, the mend will fall quite close to the rod tip. With a little practice and experimenting, you can conquer a lot of drag problems.

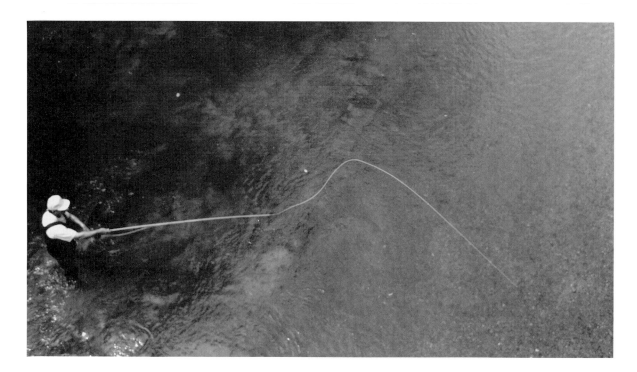

The shock wave will run down the line.

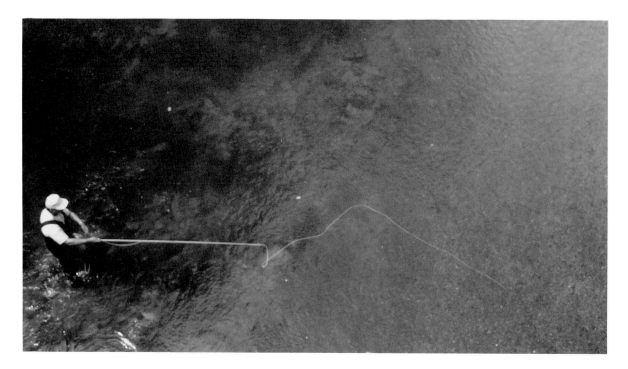

The line will fall to the water with the mend already in it.

S-Cast

This simple cast really creates a series of mends in your line. As soon as you complete the forward cast, instead of making one sharp snap with the rod, as above, give it a continuous series of quick back and forth wiggles or shakes. A succession of S-curves will form, and the line will fall to the water with enough slack so that fast water between you and the fly simply pulls out slack without pulling on the fly. This is also known as a "serpentine cast."

Many variations are possible. Suppose you are casting across a stretch of slow water but the area where the fly will land is significantly faster. If you only want slack up in the forward part of the line when it lands, shake the rod a few times quickly, as described above, and stop. Hold the rod steady while the rest of the line goes out. The line will fall to the surface as in the photograph.

If you are casting across faster water, with slower water where the fly will land, you may want all the slack curves close to you with the remainder of the line straight on the water. In such a case make your normal forward cast, stop the rod, and wait a second or two before starting the series of wiggles.

You can, depending on where the fast and slow stretches are, make your line land on the water in a variety of configurations by combining the above two maneuvers. You can put the S-curves in the front, middle, or rear section of the line. Or you can have S-curves at the front and rear of the cast with the line straight in between. Just shake the rod, stop, shake some more—all while the line is unrolling. Learn the basic S-cast and experiment.

Make a normal backcast, but aim your forward cast a little higher than usual. As soon you stop the cast, start to wiggle the rod back and forth.

Continue shaking the rod while the loop unrolls.

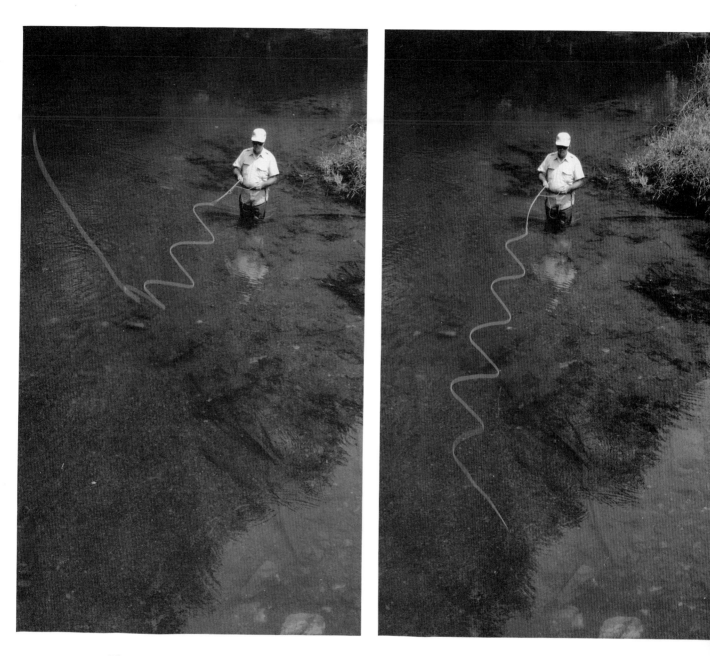

The waves will run down the entire line.

The line falls to the water with plenty of slack for a drag-free float.

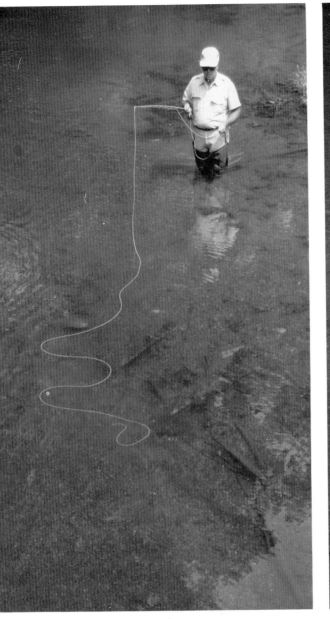

Shaking the rod two or three times and then holding it steady while the remainder of the line goes out will put slack in the forward end of the cast.

If you stop the forward cast and wait until the line is well out before shaking the rod, all the slack will fall close to you.

Stack or Puddle Cast

In dryfly fishing particularly, accuracy in the cast and slack in the drift are essential. Here is a very easy way to get both.

Cast higher than normal on the forward cast.

Just as the line is straightening out . . .

. . . lower the tip of the rod to the water.

The front end of the line will collapse with gentle curves.

A drag-free float is the result.

Aim the forward cast higher than normal.

Tug Cast

Don't confuse this with the tuck cast, which was discussed in the previous chapter. The tug cast is a slight variation of the stack cast just illustrated. Instead of simply lowering the rod tip to the water to create slack from the falling line, maintain the finishing position with the rod, but after the line straightens in the air tug it slightly with the left hand, causing it to fall back in gentle curves. The tug cast allows you a little more control in the amount of slack you create than does the stack cast.

Some fly casters recommend making a slack cast by driving a cast harder than normal and allowing the line to straighten out and bounce back so that it falls to the water in a series of curves, the so-called kick-back or bounce-back cast. The cast can be made this way, but it is far less precise than the methods I recommend above.

Just as the line straightens, give a slight tug with the left hand. Notice the left hand has pulled down a bit below the waist.

The line will fall back in gentle curves, giving a drag-free float.

Controlling Shooting Line

When you shoot line on a long cast it has a tendency to tangle if released all at once. Loops also jump up and wrap themselves around the rod blank at the end of the cast. Develop the habit of forming an O-ring with your thumb and index or middle finger to tame the line. In effect you are adding a large gathering or stripping guide.

This technique also gives greater accuracy. If you are trying to drop your fly in front of a rock forty feet away, aim downward at the target, and misjudge where you stop the tip, even by an inch or two, your line and fly may hit the water several feet short of the mark. Your presentation will also be very splashy. If, on the other hand, you overshoot the mark and don't have control of the line, you may wind up well beyond the target and perhaps in the bushes.

This is one of the great advantages to controlling the shoot as recommended. You will be amazed at how accurately—and delicately—you can drop your fly on target by aiming a few feet above the target area and merely checking the line so that it stops and drops. If short of the mark, at least the presentation is soft. If it threatens to go too far, you can stop it. With a little practice you can place your fly right on the mark nearly every time.

The stripping (or shooting) basket is an accessory used too seldom. Its main function is to make hassle-free casting possible. If you strip in a lot of line while wading a river and allow the line to be dragged downstream, it is practically impossible to make your next cast without a series of false casts, extending line a little bit at a time as you struggle with the line pulled by the current. A sinking line compounds the problem, and wading in the surf without a stripping basket can give an angler apoplexy. Waves simply wrap and tangle the line around your legs. The best solution is a basket; it keeps the line out of the water. When you cast, the line flows easily out through the guides.

If you don't have a basket, you can opt for looping line in your left hand. When you strip line, instead of allowing it to trail downstream, form a series of loops several feet long and hold them in your line hand. Make each loop a little shorter than the previous one. When you cast, simply open your hand and let the line shoot. But the basket is better still since you don't have to think about making loops and can instead concentrate on working your fly.

Whenever you release line on the forward shoot, form a ring with your thumb and first or middle finger.

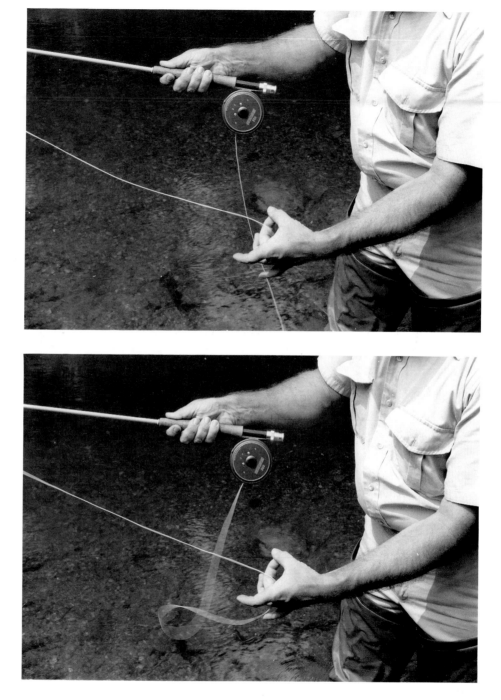

The line will not jump up and slap around the stripping guide or wrap around the rod. You can also pinch the line to stop it over the target for greater accuracy.

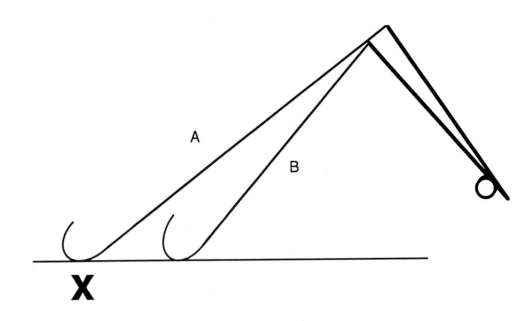

If you cast downward to drop the fly on target X and stop the tip just a few inches too low, you could present your fly with a splash several feet short.

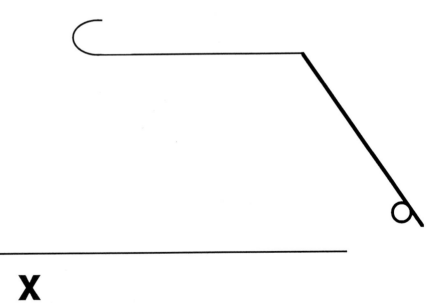

If you cast over the target and habitually control the line with your left hand, you can stop it accurately and make presentations that are more delicate.

Strip line into the basket. Stiff four-inch "fingers" of monofilament fixed in the bottom help minimize tangles.

When you cast, form an O-ring as described above to control line flow.

This helps you make tangle-free presentations.

Strip Retrieve

Although retrieving technically belongs in the area of fishing techniques rather than casting, I include it here because it presents problems for many beginning anglers and it is something many anglers do after almost every cast. Many flies, such as streamers and popping bugs, call for a strip retrieve.

With the line over the index or middle finger of the casting hand and pinched against the grip, grasp the line with your left hand—behind the casting hand as shown.

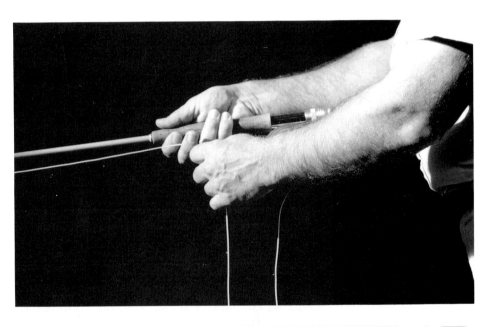

Release the pressure against the line as you begin to strip in with the left hand.

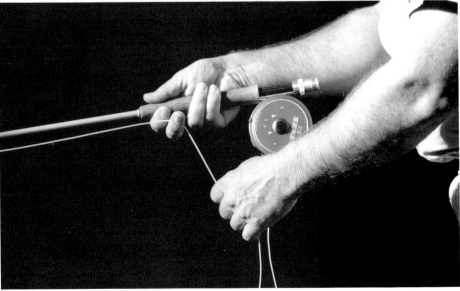

When you have stripped the fly the desired distance, pinch the line once more against the grip with your line finger.

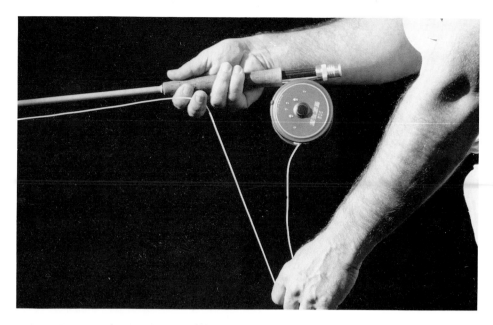

Release the line from your left hand.

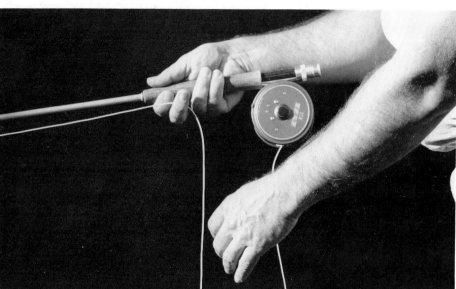

Grasp the line again behind the right hand and resume stripping.

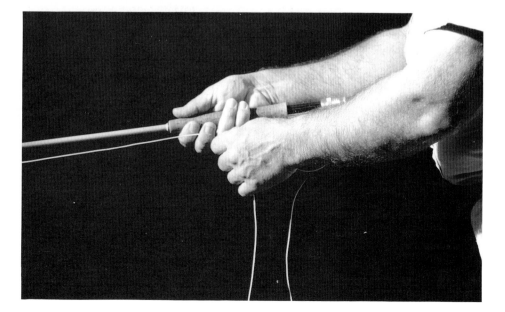

A common error to
avoid is grasping the
line ahead of the
casting hand. This
causes you to strip
the line at a sharp
angle to the
stripping guide . . .

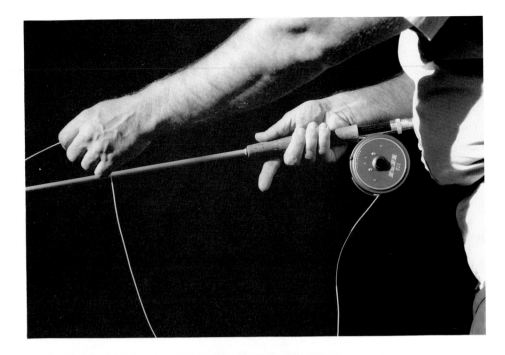

. . . and then fumble
to replace the line
over the line finger
of the rod hand.

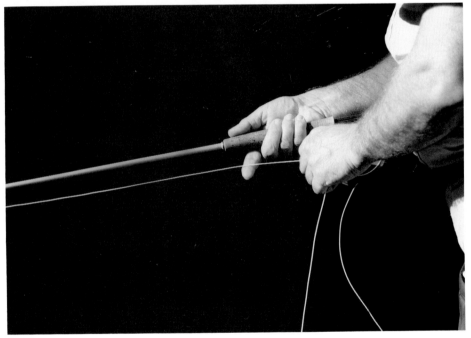

Hand-Twist Retrieve

When you want to retrieve at a different tempo, the hand-twist retrieve is useful. It provides wet flies and nymphs with a subtle twitching motion.

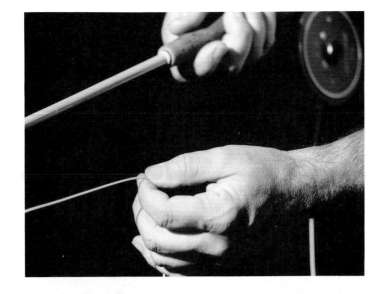

After making the cast, pinch the line between the index finger and thumb of your line hand.

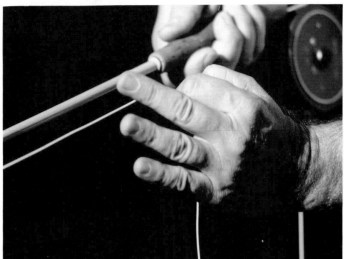

Turn your wrist back toward you while reaching out with the other three fingers of your line hand.

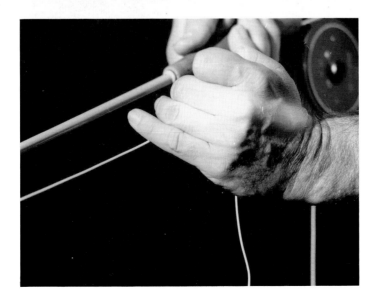

Lay your little finger over the line.

Turn your wrist back away from you so that you grip several inches of line in your hand.

Keeping this line in your palm, reach forward with the index finger and thumb.

Pinch the line as in the first photo and repeat the maneuver. After you have gathered six or more folds of line in your palm, you can simply let that line fall to the water and continue to retrieve.

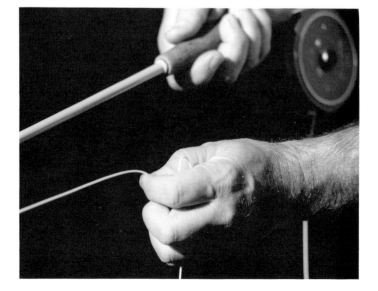

7

Problems, Faults, and Corrections

The illustrations that follow show additional common casting faults and what bad techniques and bad casts look like. They all abuse one or more of the Four Principles and waste energy. I shall explain specifically what Principles they violate and how and why each is inefficient. For visual comparison, accompanying these are photographs of improved casts that conform to the Principles. This then is a supplemental potpourri of poor casts for analysis, to teach you to see and understand what you are seeing. Focus your attention on the line in every cast; it provides the key to improvement. Gradually you will learn what to look for, to analyze casts properly, and to put your finger quickly on the source of problems.

Problem: One of the most common of all casting faults is starting with the rod in the position shown here. The rod tip must move several feet before it starts the end of the line moving. Energy is wasted just pulling out slack.

Since the rod is well back before it even starts to get loaded, there is a tendency to throw the line down behind you on the backcast . . .

. . . which may produce a weak and open backcast like that shown here.

The line often hits the water as you start the forward cast.

Remedy: Correct this cast by starting with the rod tip low to the water and no slack in the line so that 1) the end of the line gets moving right away, 2) the rod loads more quickly, and 3) the backcast can be made tighter and straighter. If you have a lot of slack on the water, strip it in or straighten it with a roll cast before beginning the backcast.

Problem: Short backcast stroke and rod stopped just past vertical. For very short casts, small flies, and ideal conditions this motion will suffice, but for longer casts it will make you work harder; it requires more force, coordination, and timing. To deal with wind or cast heavier flies, it will likewise be woefully inadequate.

Notice how short the forward motion is, due to the short backcast. The hand moves only a few inches.

Remedy: Stop the rod and casting arm farther back. A longer stroke makes the backcast easier and allows more distance for your hand to travel forward. Do the same thing if casting larger, more wind-resistant, or heavier flies.

Problem: Shock waves—or vibrations going down the line—are great energy wasters. A common cause is making a sudden, jerky acceleration, usually before the line is completely lifted from the water.

Remedy: Start slowly, progressively accelerate, and make your quickest motion just as the end of the line leaves the surface regardless of the length of line being picked up. With little apparent effort this will ensure that the rod is at maximum load when you stop it.

Problem: Here are three poor backcasts. The different loop shapes indicate that the causes are different for each. Contrary to what you might think, the rod is not too far back (at least that is not the major concern). This wide, circular loop is caused by bending the wrist while making the backcast and not accelerating during the backcast.

This cast has some acceleration and the wrist is not bent so severely, but the rod tip stopped while moving down, so the line goes down.

Note the asymmetric loop.

Here's what happens when you make a powerful backcast, expecting to load the rod, and attempt to stop the rod at one o'clock.

The force of the cast makes the rod overswing, which also throws the line downward but with a decided L-shape.

Remedy: The cure for all these faults is the same. Do not bend the wrist when you make the backcast and continually accelerate. Stop the rod by pointing or stabbing it slightly upward.

This represents poor roll-casting technique. If you start with the rod pointed nearly straight up and strike downward, the rod tip finishes moving downward, throwing the line toward the water.

The line strikes the water close to the caster. You cannot shoot any line since its forward motion is stopped and the remaining line simply rolls on the water. This makes for a splashy cast that disturbs the water.

Since so much energy is wasted by being driven down to the water, the line often fails to straighten and piles up at the end. There is a tendency now to use more power to make up for all the energy that has been wasted.

Remedy: The roll cast is merely a forward cast, so start in the same fashion, with the rod pointed farther back.

When you come forward, finish the stroke with the rod tip going forward. Don't slash down toward the water.

You will find it far easier to turn over the whole line, and it will be less likely to collapse at the end.

Problem: Perhaps the most frustrating problem of all is generally referred to as "tailing loop." The top portion of the loop drops below the bottom, and on the forward cast the line, leader, or fly generally catches the bottom portion of the loop while crossing it. Several different casting motions may result in a tailing loop, but there is a common element in all of them. Shocking the rod, unloading the rod too soon, and other actions are generally blamed for the tailing loop. Clearly the end of the line is on a collision course with the rod or forward part of the line. Since the line must follow the course of the rod tip when it stops, it must have stopped in a perfectly straight line and stayed in the way. Demonstrate this by shocking the rod as hard as you possibly can but turn the hand sharply down at the end. The cast may be awful, but the line won't tangle because the shock wasn't in fact the cause.

Remedy: Make sure you don't push or punch your hand straight ahead when you stop it; the tip of the rod must move out of the way of the line as it comes forward. You can stop the cast and instantly move the tip the slightest distance downward, but for all practical purposes the motions are so close as to be virtually one. I recommend that you think about making your final acceleration and stop with just the very slightest push down with your thumb.

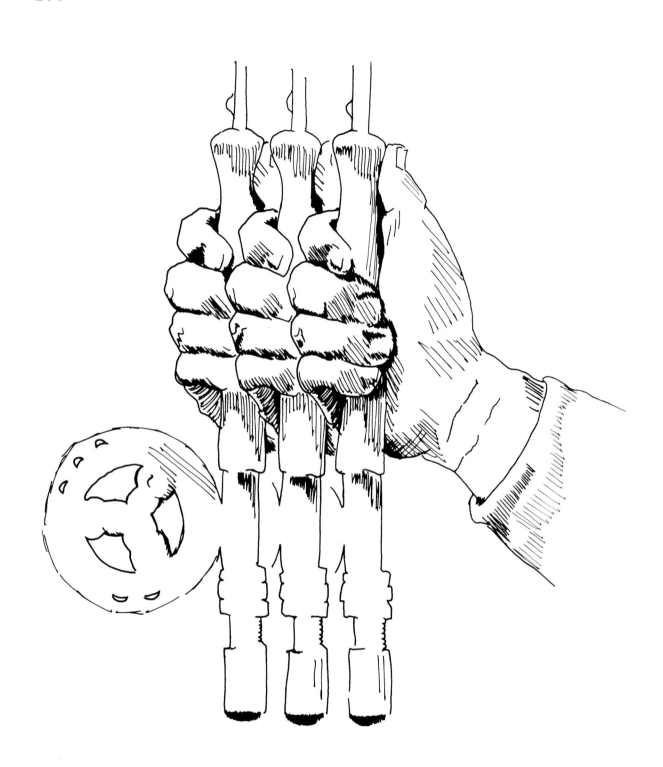

Pushing the hand straight ahead when you stop the rod will cause the rod tip to do the same. This is the cause of nearly all tailing loops.

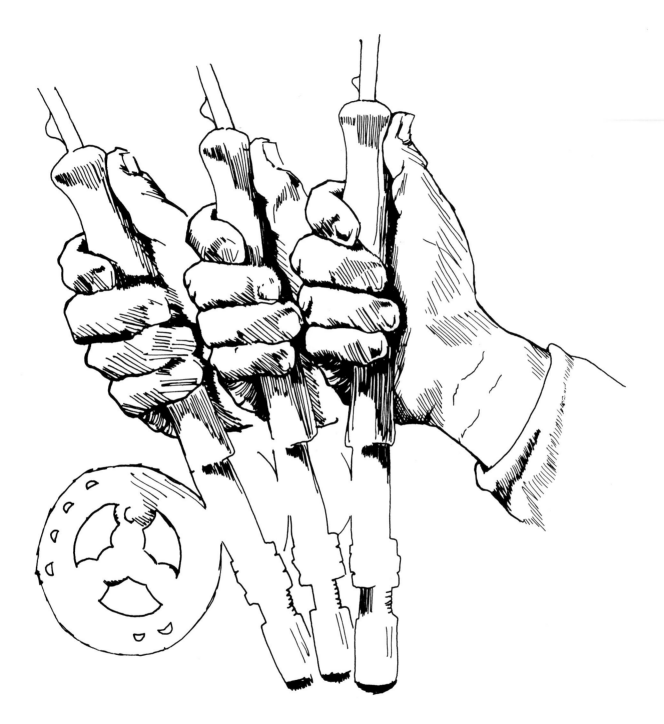

If you press down slightly with the thumb as you stop the rod, the tip will make the slightest dip and the line will not run into itself.

Problem: Here the line on the forward cast drops low and passes near the angler and may even hit him. Waiting too long or hesitating to begin the forward cast, especially if the rod is not well to the rear, will cause this problem.

Remedy: Start the forward cast sooner and constantly accelerate to a stop.

Casting With One Hand

This of course is not a fault but rather a practice procedure I recommend for correcting many problems. Many casters who have achieved some proficiency pick up bad habits from time to time. Commonly the line hand is used as a crutch and covers a sloppy or lazy rod hand. I made reference to this particularly when discussing the double haul in chapter 4. It is good to practice periodically using just one hand. Poor acceleration, jerky motions, and bad control will show up instantly when you try to make a cast without the assistance of the line hand.

210

211

Casting With the Other Hand

Another self-teaching technique. Your muscles will become so conditioned and responsive to certain motions that often it will be difficult to pinpoint the cause of a problem. If you cast with your right hand and can't analyze what is happening, try using your left. This compels you to stop and think. The muscles in your left hand, since they are not so conditioned, will not reflexively go through the motions. You will be more sensitive to the subtleties of the casting stroke.

Glossary

Acceleration. The increase in speed during the cast of 1) the rod hand or 2) the rod tip.

Aerial mend. A manipulation of the rod to create slack in the line while it is traveling forward but before it falls to the water. *See mend.*

Backcast. A cast that throws the line from a position in front of the angler to a position generally behind him.

Backhand cast. A cast made over the opposite shoulder, that is, over the left shoulder for a right-handed caster and vice versa.

Barnegat Bay cast. A cast to overcome a crosswind, which in effect uses a backcast as the forward cast.

Change-of-direction cast. A back or forward cast that finishes in a direction different from that in which it started.

Cast. The propelling of the fly line, leader, and fly by movement and flexing of the rod.

Curve cast. A cast in which the line lands curving to the right or left rather than straight ahead.

Double haul. A technique to increase line speed and rod load involving pulling the line sharply with the line hand during both the back and forward casts.

Double-taper line. A line that is of uniform diameter over nearly its entire length, tapering to a relatively fine tip at each end.

Drag. The motion of the fly moving at a speed other than that of the current in which it is traveling, caused by the pull of the line or leader.

Drift. A supplementary motion of the rod hand after the cast is finished in order to reposition the rod.

Energy. The total input of effort or work supplied by the caster in casting.

False cast. A forward cast in which the line is not allowed to fall to the water.

Force. The energy applied at any given point during the cast, inversely proportional to the length of the casting stroke.

Forward cast. A cast that throws the line from a position generally behind the angler to a position in front of him.

Galway cast. A cast using two forward casts, one to the rear of the angler, one to the front. Also called a "turn-around" or "reverse" cast.

Grasshopper cast. A horizontal forward cast in which the unrolling line lightly bounces or skips off the surface and continues to the target. Also called a "skip cast."

Grip. The 1) handle of the rod or 2) manner of holding the handle.

Haul. A sharp pull on the line with the line hand during the cast. See *double haul.*

Hook cast. A forward cast in which the line travels forward and is made to turn sharply to the right or left before falling to the water.

Launching speed. The speed at which the line commences its forward flight after the rod tip has stopped.

Line hand. The hand that holds and controls the line between the stripping guide and the reel during the cast. The left hand for right handers and vice versa. *See rod hand.*

Load. 1) The amount of resistance supplied by the weight of the line against the tip of the rod or 2) as a verb, to cause the tip to bend by moving the rod.

Loop. The convex, unrolling portion of the line traveling to the rear (in the backcast) or ahead (in the forward cast).

Mend. A technique used to create slack in the line on the water to counter the effect of drag.

Overhang. The amount of running line or shooting line between the rod tip and the rear taper of a weight-forward line or shooting taper.

Pickup. The initial part of the backcast. The raising of the rod to lift the line from the water.

Power stroke. A quick application of force near the end of the casting stroke. Also called a "power snap."

Puddle cast. See *stack cast*.

Reach cast. A forward cast that culminates in pointing and lowering the rod to the right or left after the rod's forward motion stops.

Retrieve. Drawing the fly toward the angler by pulling or manipulating the line while fishing.

Rod hand. The hand that holds and controls the rod during the cast. See *line hand*.

Roll cast. A forward cast made with the line on the water, without using a backcast.

Roll-cast pickup. Using the roll cast to get the end of the line moving and then proceeding into a regular backcast before the line can fall to the water.

Running line. The long, thin, level portion of a weight-forward fly line extending from the rear taper to the back end of the line.

S-cast. A forward cast into which the caster intentionally puts a series of zigzags or horizontal waves.

Shock waves. A series of generally vertical humps in the unrolling line that disperse and waste energy.

Shooting taper. A short fly line consisting of the belly of the line and the forward and rear tapers but not the conventional running line.

Shooting line. 1) The release of additional line to be pulled through the guides by the casting loop or 2) a thin running line attached to the rear of a shooting taper for greater casting distance.

Slack-line cast. Any cast that causes the line and leader to fall to the water with slack between the rod and the fly rather than in a straight line.

Stack cast. A cast in which the line straightens and then falls back to the water in loose waves. Also called a "puddle cast."

Stance. The position or orientation of the caster's body during the cast.

Steeple cast. A backcast made nearly vertically when obstructions prevent a normal backcast.

Stripping basket. A container worn around the waist into which line is retrieved after it has been cast. Also called a "shooting basket."

Stripping guide. The lowest and largest guide on the rod.

Stroke. The complete casting motion of the rod hand, backward or forward.

Tailing loop. A casting fault in which the top of the loop drops below the bottom of the loop and generally catches it or tangles as it crosses back upward.

Tip speed. The velocity of the rod tip during the cast.

Tip-top. The last guide at the tip of the rod.

Tuck cast. A forward cast that straightens and bounces back so that the fly enters the water while moving back toward the angler, rather than away from him.

Tug cast. A forward cast involving a slight pull with the line hand on the line once the cast has straightened in the air so that the line falls to the water with slack.

Water haul. A cast that employs water drag to load the rod deeply and for better control and distance.

Weight-forward line. A line that has most of its casting weight concentrated in a short (thirty feet or so), heavy section (called the "belly") toward the forward end.

Wind knot. An overhand knot in the line or leader caused by the same casting faults as the tailing loop.

Index